Del Monte Quality

EASY & DELICIOUS
COOKBOOK

Fruit Cocktail Cream Pie (page 180)

Del Monte Quality

EASY & DELICIOUS
COOKBOOK

BRIMAR

Created and produced by Joshua Morris Publishing, Inc.,
355 Riverside Avenue, Westport, CT 06880

Photography for this book by Eleanor Thompson.
Cover photo: Studio Tormont.
Food stylists: Robert Rall, Cathy Paukner and Karen Tack.
Grateful acknowledgment is made to Pottery Barn, Pier I, Williams-Sonoma,
Hoagland's of Greenwich, Eddie Bauer Home Collection, LCR of Westport,
Brendt Gaddy, Villeroy and Boch, Stewart Collection, Simon Pierce,
Forgotten Garden, Parc Monceau, Lexington Garden, Homespun, Complete
Kitchen, Faience, Hayday, Gargarin Antiques, Gilberti's Herb Garden,
Frances Hill Antiques, Discovery Store, Domain, The Country Store and
Lillian August for use of tableware.

Designed by Ann Beckstead.

All recipes developed and tested in the Del Monte Kitchens.

DEL MONTE, DEL MONTE LITE, FRUIT CUP, FRUIT NATURALS
and PUDDING CUP are registered trademarks of Del Monte Corporation.
FRESH CUT, GEL SNACK CUP and 2-NITE RECIPES are trademarks
Del Monte Corporation.

Published by Brimar Publishing Inc.
338 Saint Antoine St. East
Montreal, Canada H2Y 1A3
Tel. (514) 954-1441
Fax (514) 954-5086

Recipe on cover: *Sicilian Skillet Chicken* (see p. 96)
10 9 8 7 6 5 4 3 2 1

ISBN: 2-89433-185-1

CONTENTS

The Del Monte Difference

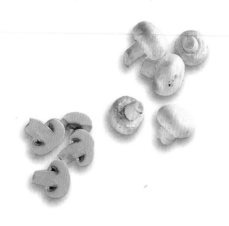

The Del Monte® name goes back more than 100 years to when the Oakland Preserving Company named their premium quality canned goods Del Monte, "from the mountain." Today, consumers know the Del Monte brand stands for premium quality, just as it did 100 years ago. When you buy Del Monte, you're buying the best.

At Del Monte, we can most of our fruits and vegetables within 24 hours of harvesting, when flavor and nutrients are at their peak. Del Monte canned fruits and vegetables are at hand and affordable year-round, when seasonal produce may be unavailable.

Fruits and vegetables packed under our label meet strict quality standards. The high heat used in the canning process preserves the food just like home canning does, *so we never need to add preservatives.*

Our cans are recyclable steel — they're made with 30% recycled steel, the maximum amount that one could use.

More than 20 years ago, Del Monte was the first company to use voluntary nutritional labeling and one of the first to comply with the new 1994 nutritional labeling regulations.

Our fruits and vegetables add variety and a balance of nutrients to your diet. These convenient products make it easy to eat your 5-A-Day. Eating 5 or more servings of fruits and vegetables daily is recommended

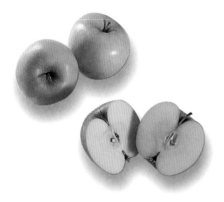

by the National Cancer Institute, the U.S. Department of Health and Human Services and the U.S. Department of Agriculture, and the National Academy of Sciences. Our fruits and vegetables make quick and tasty meals, while our convenient, shelf-stable single-serving cups make great-on-the-go snacks.

In this book you will find more than 150 recipes, perfect for today's hectic lifestyles. The book begins with our specially designed 2-NITE Recipes™. Here you will find over 50 recipes in 32 menus accompanied by dozens of additional menu suggestions and serving tips. This unique approach is presented in a "Cook Day" — "Quick Day" format which allows you to practically prepare two meals at once (for a detailed description of how this works see pages 8-11).

The second part of the book presents over 100 recipes in categories ranging from Appetizers to Desserts. Whether it's Chicken Pesto Mozzarella, Beef Quesadillas with Tomatoes and Cilantro, Pasta Pronto or Fruit Cocktail Cream Pie, you'll find a delicious solution to all your cooking problems here.

*H*ow To Make Life Easier

Commuting to work, driving the kids to soccer, balancing the checkbook — each and every day is so full, who's got time to get wholesome dinners on the table? You will — when you use Del Monte 2-NITE Recipes.

Our 2-NITE Recipes offer a flexible way for you to plan and organize your dinners.

They also help you to save time by planning two dinner menus at once. This means less time spent shopping, cooking and cleaning up.

These recipes give you a little more time for yourself. Go ahead, play tennis or take up ballroom dancing. You deserve it.

Here's what you get:

■ *More free time:* We've organized the recipe shopping lists and menus so you'll spend less time shopping, cooking and cleaning-up.

■ *Variety in meals:* We've included over 60 quick and easy recipes in the 32 menus. On pages 12-15 you'll find some quick and easy dessert recipes that can accompany any one of the menus. You'll also find additional menu suggestions throughout the 2-NITE Recipes section.

■ *Flexibility:* You design a plan to suit your lifestyle, tastes and schedule. On the "Cook Day," put together whatever recipe you choose and use the extra amounts of ingredients you cook on the "Quick Day." That "Quick Day" can be the next day the

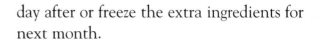

day after or freeze the extra ingredients for next month.

■ *Less Stress:* Since we've planned and organized your meals for you, you have one less thing to think about. Here's how the 2-NITE Recipe menus work:

■ *Choose a menu set.* A "Cook Day" and its accompanying "Quick Day" or any suitable Quick Day you choose.

■ *Shop once for two dinners.* Use both menus' recipe ingredient lists as a shopping list.

■ *Follow the simple step-by-step recipe instructions.*

■ *Cook a complete meal on the "Cook Day,"* cooking extra of some of these ingredients to make an entirely different menu on the "Quick Day."

■ *Take it easy on the "Quick Day!"*

Our 2-NITE Recipes and, for that matter, most recipes in this book are designed to help you get dinner on the table quickly. The recipes are simple, the ingredients are readily available and the number of pots and pans used is kept to a minimum. Here are some tips for fast and easy food preparation:

■ Keep a well-stocked pantry, refrigerator and freezer.

■ Take your shopping list to the store, so you get just what you need and don't forget anything. Buy convenience products — preseasoned canned tomatoes,

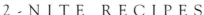

pre-shredded cheeses, pre-baked pizza crusts and pre-washed lettuce.

■ Read each recipe completely before starting. Start with the longest cooking recipe first. Don't wait around while the water boils or a dish simmers, use every spare minute to prep the next dish, load the dishwasher or clean up.

■ Rinse out bowls and pans to re-use them for several steps in a recipe. (Dishes containing raw meats, fish, poultry or eggs must be washed in hot, soapy water before re-use.)

■ Ask someone else to set the table and get the dinner beverages out.

When it comes to saving foods safely for later use, it is better to be cautious rather than casual. These general guidelines should help you make wise decisions about storing and handling foods.

■ Start with clean hands, utensils, surfaces, dishtowels and sponges.

■ Handle food as little as possible with your hands, choosing instead to mix with clean utensils.

■ Wash your hands and cutting surfaces with hot, soapy water after handling raw meats, fish and poultry, and especially before handling any foods that will not be cooked.

■ Marinate foods, covered, in the refrigerator.

■ Keeps hot foods hot (140°F), and cold foods cold (40° or below).

■ Never re-freeze foods that have thawed.

■ The more ideal the storage and handling conditions, the fresher the foods stay. Keep the refrigerator at 40°F and the freezer at 0°F. Pantry temperatures should be 65° or cooler.

■ Buy cold foods last at the store and get them home and refrigerated immediately.

Once you start cooking with our 2-NITE Recipes you'll find that you can mix and match several of the "Cook Day" — "Quick Day" combinations and even use some of your leftovers to create the "Quick Day" recipes. The more you use these recipes, the more you'll save time in the kitchen while putting delicious food on your table!

*P*each *Melba*

½ cup	seedless raspberry jam
1 can	(15¼ oz.) DEL MONTE® Yellow Cling Peach Halves, drained
1 pt.	(16 oz.) vanilla ice cream

■ In small saucepan, heat jam; set aside.

■ Place peaches in 4 serving dishes. Top with ice cream and warm jam.

4 servings

*F*ruit *'n' Yogurt*

1 can	(15 oz.) DEL MONTE® FRUIT NATURALS® (any fruit), chilled and drained
1 pt.	(16 oz.) low-fat vanilla yogurt

■ In medium bowl, combine fruit with yogurt.

4 servings

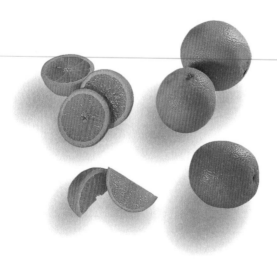

Dessert Jewels

2	DEL MONTE® GEL SNACK SNACK CUPS™, cut into cubes (any flavor)
1 can	(15¼ oz.) DEL MONTE Fruit Cocktail, drained

■ In medium bowl, toss gel with fruit.

4 servings

Pineapple Glazed Cheesecake

1 can	(8 oz.) DEL MONTE® Crushed Pineapple, undrained
⅓ cup	apricot jam or preserves
1	small (8-inch) cheesecake

■ Drain pineapple, reserving 2 tablespoons liquid.

■ In small bowl, combine reserved liquid and jam. Spoon pineapple over cheesecake; drizzle with jam mixture.

6 servings

Pudding Parfaits

4	**DEL MONTE® PUDDING CUPS®, Vanilla**
4	**DEL MONTE FRUIT CUPS®, Diced Peaches, drained**
	Non-dairy whipped topping
	Crushed cookies

■ In tall glasses, layer pudding alternately with peaches and whipped topping.

■ Sprinkle with cookies. Garnish, if desired.

4 servings

Angel Food Cake with Fruit

4 slices	**angel food cake**
1 can	**(15 oz.) DEL MONTE LITE® Chunky Mixed Fruit, chilled and drained**
6 oz.	**vanilla yogurt**

■ Top each cake slice with fruit and yogurt. Garnish, if desired.

4 servings

Apricot Foster Sundaes

1 can	**(15¼ oz.) DEL MONTE®** **Apricot Halves, undrained**
⅓ cup	**firmly packed brown sugar**
2 Tbsp.	**butter or margarine**
1 pt.	**(16 oz.) vanilla ice cream**

■ Into small saucepan, drain apricot syrup. Bring to a boil. Reduce heat to low; simmer 4 minutes.

■ Stir in sugar and butter; cook until thickened, stirring constantly. Add apricots; heat through.

■ Spoon over scoops of ice cream. Garnish, if desired.

4 servings

Peanut sauce with chicken is still the rage. When it's not too spicy, it's loved by kids and adults alike. Be sure to cook some extra chicken so you can easily make Mandarin Chicken Salad (page 19) in a day or so.

Peanut Chicken

8	half boneless chicken breasts, skinned
2 tbsp.	vegetable oil
1 can	(14½ oz.) DEL MONTE® Original Recipe Stewed Tomatoes, coarsely chopped
2	cloves garlic, minced, *or* ¼ tsp. garlic powder
¼ tsp.	ground ginger *or* 1 tsp. grated ginger root
⅛ tsp.	crushed red pepper flakes
3 tbsp.	peanut butter

■ In large skillet, cook chicken in oil over medium-high heat about 4 minutes per side or until no longer pink in center. Remove chicken from skillet. (Cool; cover and refrigerate 4 cooked chicken breasts for Quick Day, page 19.)

■ Add tomatoes, garlic, ginger and red pepper to skillet; cook 2 minutes. Stir in peanut butter.

■ Return chicken to skillet; heat through. Sprinkle with chopped cilantro and peanuts, if desired.

4 servings

Prep time: *4 minutes*
Cook time: *12 minutes*

DO-AHEAD NOTE:
Cook extra chicken.

<u>SERVE PEANUT CHICKEN WITH:</u>

Garlic Green Beans
1 can   (14½ oz.) DEL MONTE Whole Green Beans, drained
2 tsp.   butter or margarine
2   cloves garlic, minced, or
     ¼ tsp. garlic powder

In small saucepan, cook green beans with butter and garlic until heated through.
4 servings

Parsley Rice
Whole Wheat Dinner Rolls

This yummy chicken salad is a cinch to make—no pots to clean, no waiting for the chicken to cool—since the chicken is cooked ahead on Cook Day (page 16).

Mandarin Chicken Salad

1 can	(15½ oz.) **DEL MONTE®** **Pineapple Chunks in Heavy Syrup, undrained**
3 tbsp.	**vegetable oil**
3 tbsp.	**cider vinegar**
1 tbsp.	**soy sauce**
4 cups	**shredded cabbage** *or* **iceberg lettuce**
1 can	(14½ oz.) **DEL MONTE Fresh Cut Diced Tomatoes, drained**
4	**cooked half boneless chicken breasts**
⅓ cup	**packed cilantro, chopped,** *or* **½ cup sliced green onions**

■ Drain pineapple, reserving ¼ cup syrup. In small bowl, combine reserved syrup, oil, vinegar and soy sauce; stir briskly with fork.

■ In large bowl, toss cabbage with pineapple, tomatoes, chicken (cooked on Cook Day, page 16) and cilantro. Add dressing as desired; gently toss.

■ Sprinkle with toasted slivered almonds, crumbled dry noodles (from Oriental noodle soup mix) or toasted sesame seeds, if desired.

4 servings

Prep time: 15 minutes

SERVE MANDARIN CHICKEN SALAD WITH:

Rice Cakes or Bread

This recipe could hardly be easier, but if extra chicken is baked with it, Country Chicken and Biscuits (page 23) is even simpler.

Chicken Parmesan Noodle Bake

1 pkg.	**(12 oz.) extra wide noodles**
8	**half boneless chicken breasts, skinned**
½ tsp.	**rosemary, crushed**
2 cans	**(14½ oz. *each*) DEL MONTE® Italian Recipe Stewed Tomatoes**
½ cup	**(2 oz.) shredded mozzarella cheese**
¼ cup	**(1 oz.) grated Parmesan cheese**

■ Preheat oven to 450°F.

■ Cook noodles according to package directions; drain.

■ Meanwhile, sprinkle chicken with rosemary; season with salt and pepper, if desired. Arrange chicken in 13 x 9-inch baking dish. Bake, uncovered, 20 minutes or until chicken is no longer pink in center. Drain; remove chicken from dish. (Cool; cover and refrigerate 4 cooked chicken breasts for Quick Day, page 23.)

■ Drain tomatoes, reserving liquid. In large bowl, toss reserved liquid with noodles; place in baking dish. Top with chicken and tomatoes. Sprinkle with cheeses.

■ Bake 10 minutes or until heated through. Sprinkle with additional Parmesan cheese and garnish, if desired.

4 servings

Prep and bake time: 35 minutes

DO-AHEAD NOTE:
Bake extra chicken.

<u>SERVE CHICKEN PARMESAN NOODLE BAKE WITH:</u>

Crisp Green Salad
6 cups chopped lettuce
1   small red onion, sliced
          Creamy Italian dressing
In large bowl, toss lettuce and onion with dressing.

4 to 6 servings

Crusty French Bread

If you have a well-stocked pantry and keep cooked chicken in the freezer, you'll be able to toss this menu together anytime. If everyone wants pizza instead, use this chicken in place of turkey and make Rosemary Turkey Pizza (page 155).

Country Chicken and Biscuits

1 can	(10¾ oz.) condensed cream of celery soup
⅓ cup	milk or water
4	half chicken breasts, cooked and cut bite-size
1 can	(14½ oz.) DEL MONTE® Cut Green Beans, drained
1 can	(11 oz.) refrigerated biscuits

■ Preheat oven to 375°F.

■ In large bowl, combine soup and milk. Gently stir in chicken (cooked on Cook Day, page 20) and green beans; season with pepper, if desired. Spoon into 11 x 7-inch microwavable dish.

■ Cover with plastic wrap; slit to vent. Microwave on HIGH 8 to 10 minutes or until heated through, rotating once. If using a conventional oven, cover with foil and bake at 375°F, 20 to 25 minutes or until hot.

■ Separate biscuit dough into individual biscuits. Immediately arrange biscuits over hot mixture. Bake in conventional oven about 15 minutes or until biscuits are golden brown and baked through.

4 servings

Prep and cook time: 30 minutes

SERVE COUNTRY CHICKEN AND BISCUITS WITH:

Chilled DEL MONTE Pineapple Slices
or
Tossed Green Salad

Cook sausage and extra chicken and rice to make Tomato Chicken Gumbo
(page 27) later.

Hot & Spicy Buffalo Chicken Wings

1 can	**(15 oz.) DEL MONTE® Original Sloppy Joe Sauce**
¼ cup	**DEL MONTE Thick & Chunky Salsa, Medium**
1 tbsp.	**cider vinegar**
20	**chicken wings (about 4 lb.)**
6	**chicken thighs**
½ lb.	**hot sausage links or Polish sausage**

■ Preheat oven to 400°F.

■ In small bowl, combine sloppy joe sauce, salsa and vinegar; cover and refrigerate ¼ of mixture to serve with cooked chicken wings. Set aside remaining sauce mixture to brush over chicken wings as they cook.

■ Arrange wings in single layer in large, shallow baking pan; brush both sides of chicken wings with sauce mixture.

■ On middle rack in oven, bake chicken wings, uncovered, 35 minutes or until chicken is no longer pink in center, turning and brushing with remaining sauce mixture after 15 minutes.

■ Pre-bake sausage and thighs at same time, see Tips. (Cool; cover and refrigerate cooked sausage and thighs for Quick Day, page 27.) Serve wings with reserved ¼ cup sauce.

4 servings

Prep time:	*5 minutes*
Cook time:	*35 minutes*

SERVE HOT & SPICY BUFFALO CHICKEN WINGS WITH:

Hot Buttered Rice
2 cups uncooked long-grain
        white rice
1 tbsp. butter *or* margarine
1 tsp. basil *or* thyme, crushed
        (optional)

Cook rice according to package directions. (Cool; cover and refrigerate 1½ cups cooked rice for Quick Day, page 27.) Toss remaining rice with butter and basil.

4 servings

Tossed Green Salad

TIPS:
• *To pre-bake sausage and thighs, arrange in large, shallow baking pan. Place, uncovered, below pan of tonight's Buffalo Chicken Wings and bake 35 minutes or until chicken is no longer pink in center.*
• *Marinade that has come into contact with raw meat must be boiled a few minutes before serving.*

*The chicken, sausage and rice are cooked on Cook Day (page 24) to make this gumbo.
Or, if you're in the mood for something else, use these thighs (boned) and sausage to replace
the beef in Beef Steak Chili (page 43). Just freeze this cooked rice for another day.*

*T*omato Chicken Gumbo

1 can	**(14 oz.) chicken broth**
½ lb.	**hot sausage links *or* Polish sausage cooked and sliced**
1½ cups	**cooked white rice**
1 can	**(26 oz.) DEL MONTE® Traditional *or* Chunky Garlic and Herb Spaghetti Sauce**
6	**chicken thighs, cooked, skinned, boned and cubed**
1 can	**(11 oz.) DEL MONTE Summer Crisp Corn, drained**
1	**green bell pepper, diced**

■ In 6-quart pot, bring broth and 2 cups water to a boil; add sausage links, rice and chicken thighs (cooked on Cook Day, page 24). Add all remaining ingredients. Cover; cook over medium heat 10 minutes or until heated through.

■ Add additional water or broth for a thinner gumbo. For spicier gumbo, serve with hot red pepper sauce.

4 servings (about 2½ cups each)

Prep and cook time: 15 minutes

SERVE TOMATO CHICKEN GUMBO WITH:

Hot Biscuits or Dinner Rolls

This chicken is great right off the grill or tasty later in salads, sandwiches or almost any recipe calling for cooked chicken. Grill extra to make Grilled Chicken Taco Salad (page 31).

Hickory BBQ *Chicken*

1 can	**(15 oz.) DEL MONTE® Hickory Sloppy Joe Sauce**
¼ cup	**fresh lime juice**
8	**half boneless chicken breasts, skinned**

■ Set aside ½ cup sauce to serve over cooked chicken; cover and refrigerate until 30 minutes before serving. Stir lime juice into remaining sauce in can. Arrange chicken in 11 x 7-inch dish. Cover with sauce mixture; turn to coat. Cover and refrigerate at least 30 minutes or overnight.

■ Grill chicken over hot coals (or broil) 4 minutes per side or until no longer pink in center, brushing chicken occasionally with marinade. (Cool; cover and refrigerate 4 cooked chicken breasts for Quick Day, page 31.)

■ Serve remaining chicken with reserved ½ cup sauce. (Any remaining marinade must be cooked for several minutes before serving with chicken.)

4 servings

Prep time:	5 minutes
Marinate time:	30 minutes
Cook time:	10 minutes

SERVE HICKORY BBQ CHICKEN WITH:

Warm French Bread
Marinated Corn and Pepper Salad

1 can	(11 oz.) DEL MONTE Summer Crisp Corn, drained
½	red or green bell pepper, diced
2	green onions, sliced
	Oil and vinegar dressing

In medium bowl, combine corn, pepper and onions; toss with dressing. Garnish, if desired.

4 servings

TIP:
Start the coals in the barbecue about 40 minutes before you plan to cook.

DO-AHEAD NOTE:
Grill extra chicken.

*Grill extra chicken on Cook Day (page 28) to add to this salad at the end of a busy day.
Or, if you want something hot, make Beef Steak Chili (page 43) instead,
substituting this chicken for beef.*

Grilled Chicken Taco Salad

1 can	**(14½ oz.) DEL MONTE® Mexican Recipe Stewed Tomatoes**
⅓ cup	**DEL MONTE Picante Sauce, Hot**
2 tbsp.	**vegetable oil**
2 tbsp.	**vinegar, such as red wine *or* cider**
1	**large head romaine lettuce, chopped (about 10 to 12 cups)**
4	**half boneless chicken breasts, grilled and cut bite-size**
1 can	**(8 oz.) kidney beans, drained (optional)**
1 cup	**(4 oz.) shredded sharp Cheddar cheese**
3 cups	**broken tortilla chips**

■ Drain tomatoes, reserving 1 tablespoon liquid. Chop tomatoes; set aside.

■ In small bowl, make dressing by blending reserved tomato liquid, picante sauce, oil and vinegar; stir briskly with fork.

■ In large bowl, toss lettuce with reserved tomatoes, chicken (cooked on Cook Day, page 28), beans and cheese. Add dressing as desired. Add chips; toss. Season with salt and pepper, if desired. Serve immediately. Garnish, if desired.

4 main-dish servings

Prep time: 15 minutes

TIP:
Add avocado, green onions, olives, corn, radishes or cilantro, if desired.

SERVE GRILLED CHICKEN
TACO SALAD WITH:

*Hot Buttered Flour Tortillas
(Microwave)*

**Flour tortillas
Butter or margarine**

Wrap desired number of tortillas in plastic wrap. Microwave on HIGH 15 seconds or until warm. Or, wrap in foil and heat in conventional oven at 350°F, 5 to 7 minutes or until warm.

Italian style stewed tomatoes, garlic and bacon make this quick-to-fix dish rich and flavorful.
Cook double the amount of chicken and rice, and a second meal (page 35)
is ready in no time.

Mediterranean Chicken

4 slices	bacon, diced
8	half boneless chicken breasts, skinned
1 can	(14½ oz.) DEL MONTE® Italian Recipe Stewed Tomatoes
6	medium pitted black olives, cut into quarters (optional)
2	large cloves garlic, minced *or* ¼ tsp. garlic powder

■ In large skillet, cook bacon over medium-high heat 2 minutes (bacon will not be done); remove bacon from skillet, reserving drippings in skillet.

■ Flatten chicken slightly with palm of hand; season with salt and pepper, if desired. Place 4 chicken breasts in bacon drippings in skillet; cook 6 minutes on each side or until chicken is no longer pink in center. (Cool; cover and refrigerate cooked chicken for Quick Day, page 35.)

■ Return bacon to skillet. Add remaining 4 chicken breasts; cook 6 minutes on each side or until bacon is crisp and chicken is no longer pink in center.

■ Add tomatoes, olives and garlic to skillet; cook, uncovered, about 5 minutes or until slightly thickened.

4 servings

Prep time:	5 minutes
Cook time:	30 minutes

DO-AHEAD NOTE:
Cook extra chicken and rice.

SERVE MEDITERRANEAN CHICKEN WITH:

Confetti Rice

2½ cups	uncooked long-grain white rice
1 can	(8½ oz.) DEL MONTE Peas and Carrots, drained
2 tbsp.	butter or margarine
2 tbsp.	chopped parsley

In medium saucepan, cook rice according to package directions. (Cool, cover and refrigerate 3 to 4 cups cooked rice for Quick Day, page 35.) Stir vegetables, butter and parsley into remaining rice; heat through.

4 servings

Bread Sticks

There isn't a quicker stir-fry, since you cook the chicken and rice ahead (page 32).
Use less red pepper for a milder dish or more for a fiery one.

Sweet and Spicy Chicken Stir-Fry

1 can	(8 oz.) DEL MONTE® Pineapple Chunks In Its Own Juice, undrained
2 tsp.	vegetable oil
1	large green bell pepper, cut into stirps
4	half boneless chicken breasts, skinned, cooked and cubed
¾ cup	sweet and sour sauce
¼ tsp.	crushed red pepper flakes
3 cups	cooked rice

■ Drain pineapple, reserving ⅓ cup juice.

■ In large skillet, heat oil over medium-high heat. Add green pepper; stir-fry 2 minutes.

■ Add chicken (cooked on Cook Day, page 32), sweet and sour sauce, red pepper flakes, pineapple and reserved juice; stir-fry 3 minutes or until heated through.

■ Meanwhile, place rice (cooked on Cook Day, page 32) in microwavable dish; sprinkle with 2 teaspoons water. Cover with plastic wrap; slit to vent.

■ Microwave on HIGH 4 minutes or until heated through. Spoon onto serving plate; top with chicken mixture. (If microwave is not available, see Tips.)

4 servings

Prep time:	*5 minutes*
Cook time:	*5 minutes*

SERVE SWEET AND SPICY CHICKEN STIR-FRY WITH:

Garlic Green Beans

TIPS:
• *Look for sweet and sour sauce in the international section of the supermarket.*
• *If microwave is not available to reheat rice: In 3-quart saucepan, bring ⅓ cup water to boil; add rice. Cover and cook over low heat, stirring occasionally, about 10 minutes or until heated through. (Rice scorches easily, so avoid high heat.)*

The aroma of the herbed chicken cooking will bring the family in before you have a chance to announce dinner is ready. Cook some extra chicken for the Quick Day (page 39).

Rosemary Chicken and Vegetables

4	carrots, cut into thick julienne strips
3	baking potatoes, cut bite-size
1½ tsp.	garlic salt, divided
½ tsp.	rosemary leaves, crushed, divided
3 lb.	cut-up chicken, skin trimmed
4	half chicken breasts

■ Preheat oven to 400°F.

■ In 13 x 9-inch or 3-quart baking dish, combine vegetables with ½ teaspoon garlic salt and ¼ teaspoon rosemary. Arrange all of the chicken over vegetables; sprinkle with remaining 1 teaspoon garlic salt and ¼ teaspoon rosemary. Season with salt and pepper, if desired.

■ Bake 30 to 40 minutes or until chicken is no longer pink in center, and vegetables are tender. (Cool; cover and refrigerate 4 chicken breasts for Quick Day, page 39.)

■ Garnish if desired.

4 to 6 servings

Prep time:	5 minutes
Bake time:	40 minutes

TIP:
Be sure to buy the groceries for both the Cook and Quick Days.

DO-AHEAD NOTE:
Cook extra chicken.

SERVE ROSEMARY CHICKEN AND VEGETABLES WITH:

Pear Spinach Salad
4 cups torn spinach leaves
1 can (15 oz.) DEL MONTE® Lite Sliced Pears, drained
⅓ cup thinly sliced green onions
Italian dressing
In large bowl, toss spinach, pears and onions with enough dressing to coat.
4 servings

Dinner Rolls

Already baked chicken reheats nicely in this microwave recipe. And dinner's a lot less fussy when the chicken is already cooked! If you prefer, you may use this chicken instead of tuna to make Tarragon Tuna Pasta Salad (page 71).

*S*killet Ranch Chicken *(Microwave)*

1	onion, chopped
1 tbsp.	vegetable oil
1 can	(14½ oz.) DEL MONTE® Italian or Original Recipe Stewed Tomatoes
½ tsp.	thyme, crushed
4	half chicken breasts, baked and skinned
1 can	(15¼ oz.) DEL MONTE Sweet Peas, drained
1 can	(10¾ oz.) condensed cream of celery soup

■ In large skillet, cook onion in oil over medium heat until tender. Stir in tomatoes and thyme. Cook, stirring occasionally, until thickened; keep warm.

■ Arrange chicken (cooked on Cook Day, page 36) in shallow microwavable dish; cover. Microwave on HIGH 4 to 5 minutes or until heated through.

■ Just before serving, stir peas and soup into skillet; heat through. Add chicken; spoon sauce over chicken.

4 servings

Prep and cook time: *16 minutes*

SERVE SKILLET RANCH CHICKEN
WITH:

Buttermilk Biscuits

Dilled Carrot Salad

¼ tsp. dill weed

1 can (8¼ oz.) DEL MONTE Sliced Carrots, drained

5 cups torn romaine lettuce
Dijon dressing

In large bowl, sprinkle dill over carrots. Add lettuce; toss with dressing.

4 servings

For another meal, cook an extra pound of steak to make Beef Steak Chili (page 43).

Grilled Steak

2½ lb. **beef steak, such as flank, sirloin *or* round steak**

Garlic salt

Pepper

■ Season meat with garlic salt and pepper. Grill over hot coals (or broil) about 5 minutes per side or until desired doneness is reached.

■ Cut meat diagonally across grain into thin slices. (Cool; cover and refrigerate 1 pound cooked meat for Quick Day, page 43.)

4 servings

Prep and cook time: 10 minutes

DO-AHEAD NOTE:
Cook extra steak.

SERVE GRILLED STEAK WITH:

*Spinach Salad with Pears
and Red Onions*

6 cups torn spinach leaves
1 can (15¼ oz.) DEL MONTE®
Sliced Pears, drained
½ red onion, sliced
Oil and vinegar dressing

In large bowl, toss spinach, pears and onion with dressing.

4 to 6 servings

*Baked Potatoes with Sour Cream
and Chives*

For easy chili making, plan to toss an extra steak on the grill a day or two ahead. Rather have salad? Make Mandarin Chicken Salad (page 19) using this cooked steak instead of chicken.

Beef Steak Chili

2 cans	(14½ oz. *each*) DEL MONTE® Chili Style Chunky Tomatoes
1 can	(15 oz.) black *or* kidney beans, rinsed and drained
1 lb.	grilled beef steak slices, cubed
1 can	(8¾ oz.) DEL MONTE Whole Kernel Corn, drained
2 tbsp.	fresh lime juice

■ In large skillet, cook tomatoes and beans over medium-high heat 5 minutes or until slightly thickened, stirring occasionally.

■ Stir in meat (cooked on Cook Day, page 40), corn and lime juice; heat through. Season with salt and pepper, if desired.

■ Sprinkle with chopped cilantro, if desired.

4 servings

Prep and cook time: 15 minutes

TIP:
For a spicier chili, add chili powder, cayenne pepper or hot pepper sauce.

SERVE BEEF STEAK CHILI WITH:

Pineapple Spritzer
Ice
DEL MONTE Pineapple
Juice, chilled
Sparkling water

For each serving, fill tall glass with ice. Fill with ¾ juice and ¼ water.

Corn Bread or French Bread

*While preparing tonight's beef stir-fry, place half of the steak in a marinade
and refrigerate for your next night's dinner (page 47).*

Stir-Fry Tomato Beef

2 cups	uncooked long-grain white rice
2 lb.	flank steak
1 tbsp.	cornstarch
1 tbsp.	soy sauce
2	cloves garlic, minced
1 tsp.	minced ginger root *or* ¼ tsp. ground ginger
1 tbsp.	vegetable oil
1 can	(14½ oz.) DEL MONTE® Original Recipe Stewed Tomatoes

■ Cook rice according to package directions. (Cool; cover and refrigerate half of cooked rice for Quick Day, page 47.) Keep remaining rice hot.

■ Cut meat crosswise into 2 equal pieces, about 1 pound each. (Cover and marinate 1 pound of meat in refrigerator overnight for Quick Day, page 47.) Cut remaining meat in half lengthwise, and then cut crosswise into thin slices.

■ In medium bowl, combine cornstarch, soy sauce, garlic and ginger. Add sliced meat; toss to coat.

■ Preheat oil in large skillet over high heat. Cook meat in oil, stirring constantly, until browned. Add tomatoes; cook until thickened, about 5 minutes, stirring frequently.

■ Serve over hot rice. Garnish with chopped cilantro or green onions, if desired.

4 to 6 servings

Prep time:	*10 minutes*
Cook time:	*15 minutes*

TIPS:
• *Partially freeze the meat for easier slicing.*
• *After extra rice is cooked, cover loosely and refrigerate. Rice may be frozen for several months in a tightly sealed freezer bag.*

DO-AHEAD NOTE:
Marinate flank steak.

Nothing is tastier than meat that marinates overnight!

Marinated Flank Steak with Pineapple

1 can	(15¼ oz.) **DEL MONTE®** **Pineapple Slices In Its Own Juice, undrained**
¼ cup	**teriyaki sauce**
2 tbsp.	**honey**
1 lb.	**flank steak**

SERVE MARINATED FLANK STEAK WITH PINEAPPLE WITH:

Sesame Rice
(Microwave)

3 cups cooked long-grain white rice
2   green onions, sliced
2 tbsp. toasted sesame seeds

In 1½ -quart microwavable dish, toss rice (cooked on Cook Day, page 44), 2 teaspoons water, onions and sesame seeds. Cover and microwave on HIGH 2 to 3 minutes.

4 servings

Honey Mustard Carrots
(Microwave)

1 tbsp. honey
1 tsp. Dijon mustard
1 can (14½ oz.) DEL MONTE Sliced Carrots, drained

In 1-quart microwavable dish, combine honey and mustard. Add carrots. Cover and microwave on HIGH 2 to 3 minutes.

4 servings

■ (If meat was marinated on Cook Day, page 44, go to next step.) For marinade, drain pineapple, reserving 2 tablespoons juice. Set pineapple aside. In shallow 2-quart dish, combine reserved juice, teriyaki sauce and honey; mix well. Add meat; turn to coat. Cover and refrigerate at least 30 minutes or overnight. Remove meat from marinade, reserving marinade.

■ Grill meat over hot coals (or broil), brushing occasionally with marinade. Cook about 4 minutes per side for rare; about 5 minutes per side for medium; or 6 minutes per side for well done.

■ During last 4 minutes of cooking, brush pineapple slices with marinade; grill until heated through.

■ Slice meat across grain; serve with pineapple.

4 servings

Prep time:	5 minutes
Marinate time:	30 minutes
Cook time:	10 minutes

TIPS:

• *Sprinkle cold rice with a teaspoon of water, and then cover tightly with vented plastic wrap before reheating in the microwave.*
• *Marinade that has come into contact with raw meat must be cooked several minutes before serving.*

Cooked under the broiler or over hot coals, these kabobs are delicious!
Save half of the grilled meat for Quick Day (page 51).

Beef Kabobs with Apricot Glaze

2 lb.	sirloin steak
1 can	(15¼ oz.) DEL MONTE® Apricot Halves, undrained
1 tbsp.	cornstarch
1 tsp.	Dijon mustard
½ tsp.	basil, crushed
1	small green bell pepper, cut into ¾-inch pieces
4	medium mushrooms, cut in half
4 to 8	skewers

■ Cut meat into 2 equal portions. Cut 1 portion into 1½-inch cubes; set aside remaining portion.

■ Drain apricot syrup into a small saucepan. Blend in cornstarch until dissolved. Cook over medium heat, stirring constantly, until thickened. Stir in mustard and basil. Set aside.

■ Thread meat cubes, apricots, green pepper and mushrooms alternately onto skewers; brush with apricot mixture before and during cooking.

■ Grill kabobs and the reserved 1-lb. piece of meat over hot coals (or broil), about 5 minutes per side or to desired doneness. (Cool; cover and refrigerate extra piece of cooked meat for Quick Day, page 51.) Garnish, if desired.

4 servings

Prep time:	*10 minutes*
Cook time:	*15 minutes*

SERVE BEEF KABOBS WITH:

Hot Cooked Rice
¾ cup uncooked long-grain white rice
1 tbsp. butter or margarine
Cook rice according to package directions. Toss rice with butter.
4 servings

TIP:
To prevent burning of wood skewers, soak them in water for 10 minutes before assembling kabobs.

DO-AHEAD NOTE:
Cook extra steak and rice.

This stuffed potato is a meal in itself. It's especially quick since it uses meat grilled on Cook Day (page 48). Or, make Grilled Chicken Taco Salad (page 31) using this beef instead of chicken.

Stroganoff Stuffed Potatoes *(Microwave)*

4	**medium baking potatoes**
1	**onion, chopped**
6	**medium mushrooms, sliced**
1 tbsp.	**butter** *or* **margarine**
1 lb.	**grilled sirloin steak, cut bite-size**
1 can	**(14½ oz.) DEL MONTE® Mixed Vegetables, drained**
1 cup	**sour cream**

■ Pierce each potato with a fork; place on paper towel in microwave oven. Microwave on HIGH about 16 minutes or until tender, rotating once.

■ In large skillet on stovetop, cook onion and mushrooms in butter until tender. Add meat (cooked on Cook Day, page 48) and vegetables; heat through. Remove from heat; stir in sour cream.

■ Split tops of potatoes; fluff insides with fork. Season potatoes with salt and pepper, if desired. Spoon meat mixture over potatoes.

4 servings

Prep time:	5 minutes
Cook time:	16 minutes

HEALTHY HINT:
Substitute light or nonfat sour cream; use a nonstick skillet and reduce butter.

Thick, juicy pork chops smothered in a tasty Italian sauce, who could resist?
Save some of these chops to make Pork Fried Rice (page 55).

*I*talian Pork Chops

4 cups	uncooked long-grain white rice
8	large (½-inch thick) pork chops
1 tsp.	basil, crushed
1 can	(26 oz.) DEL MONTE® Spaghetti Sauce with Mushrooms *or* Chunky Italian Herb Spaghetti Sauce
1	green bell pepper, cut into thin strips

■ Cook rice according to package directions. (Cool; cover and refrigerate 7 to 8 cups cooked rice for Quick Day, page 55.) Keep remaining rice hot.

■ Preheat broiler. Sprinkle meat with basil; season with salt and pepper, if desired. Place meat on broiler pan. Broil 4 inches from heat about 6 minutes per side or until no longer pink in center. (Cool; cover and refrigerate 4 chops for Quick Day, page 55.) Keep remaining chops warm.

■ In 11 x 7-inch microwavable dish, combine sauce and bell pepper. Cover with plastic wrap; slit to vent. Microwave on HIGH 5 to 6 minutes or until peppers are tender-crisp and sauce is heated through. Add meat; cover with sauce. Microwave 1 minute. Serve over hot rice.

4 servings

Prep and cook time: 25 minutes

TIP:
When extra meat and rice stop steaming, cover loosely and refrigerate.

DO-AHEAD NOTE:
Cook extra pork chops and rice.

SERVE ITALIAN PORK CHOPS WITH:

Savory Mixed Vegetables
1 can   (14½ oz.) DEL MONTE Mixed Vegetables, drained
2 tsp.   butter or margarine
¼ tsp.   oregano, crushed
Dash garlic powder

In small saucepan, cook vegetables with butter, oregano and garlic powder over medium heat until heated through, stirring occasionally.

4 servings

Fried Rice is a dish almost everyone loves. This version makes an especially easy weeknight supper, since the meat and rice are cooked ahead on Cook Day (page 52). Or, this pork could be used instead of chicken to make Mandarin Chicken Salad (page 19).

*P*ork Fried Rice

1	onion, finely chopped
2 tbsp.	vegetable oil
7 cups	cooked rice (about 2½ cups uncooked rice)
4	cooked pork chops, diced
1 can	(14½ oz.) DEL MONTE® Peas and Carrots, drained
3	green onions, sliced
3 tbsp.	soy sauce

■ In large skillet or wok, cook onion in hot oil until tender-crisp.

■ Add cooked rice (cooked on Cook Day, page 52); cook over medium heat 8 minutes or until heated through, stirring frequently.

■ Stir in meat (cooked on Cook Day, page 52), vegetables and soy sauce; heat through. Season with pepper, if desired.

4 servings

Prep and cook time: 15 minutes

SERVE PORK FRIED RICE WITH:

Spinach Pineapple Salad
6 cups torn spinach leaves
1 can   (8 oz.) DEL MONTE
       Pineapple Tidbits In Its Own
       Juice, drained
       Oil and vinegar dressing

In large bowl, toss spinach and pineapple with dressing.

4 to 6 servings

This dinner is tasty and quick. Country Skillet Hash (page 59) will be every bit as good, but even easier since you cook the meat for it tonight.

Louisiana Pork Chops

2 tsp.	garlic powder
½ tsp.	*each* black pepper, white pepper and cayenne
8	pork chops (¾ inch thick)
2 tbsp.	butter *or* margarine
1 can	(14½ oz.) DEL MONTE® Cajun *or* Original Recipe Stewed Tomatoes

■ In small bowl, combine garlic powder and peppers; rub into both sides of meat. In large skillet, heat butter over medium-high heat. Add meat; cook 5 minutes on each side. Drain. (Cool; cover and refrigerate 4 cooked chops for Quick Day, page 59.)

■ Add tomatoes to skillet; reduce heat to medium. Cover; cook until meat is no longer pink in center, about 10 minutes. Remove meat to serving dish; keep warm.

■ In same skillet, cook tomatoes over medium-high heat until thickened, stirring occasionally; spoon over meat.

4 servings

Prep time:	*5 minutes*
Cook time:	*20 minutes*

TIP:
Look for the economical "family pack" pork chops offered at some meat counters. You often save by buying the larger quantity.

DO-AHEAD NOTE:
Cook extra pork chops.

SERVE LOUISIANA PORK CHOPS WITH:

Corn Nugget Cornbread Stuffing
Cornbread stuffing mix (see package for additional required ingredients)
1 can (15¼ oz.) DEL MONTE Whole Kernel Corn, drained
Prepare 4 servings stuffing according to package directions. Add corn; toss. Heat according to stuffing mix package directions.
4 servings

Tossed Green Salad

*As quick as it is tasty, this hash is made from already cooked pork chops (page 56).
Stewed tomatoes give this dish a new twist.*

Country Skillet Hash

1	**medium onion, chopped**
2	**cloves garlic, minced**
2 tbsp.	**butter** *or* **margarine**
1 can	**(14½ oz.) DEL MONTE® Whole New Potatoes, drained and diced**
1 can	**(14½ oz.) DEL MONTE Original Recipe Stewed Tomatoes**
4	**pork chops (¾-inch thick), cooked and diced**
1	**green bell pepper, chopped**
½ tsp.	**thyme, crushed**

■ In large skillet, cook onion and garlic in butter over medium heat until tender; add potatoes, tomatoes, meat (cooked on Cook Day, page 56), green pepper and thyme. Cook 5 minutes, stirring frequently.

■ Season with salt and black pepper, if desired.

4 servings

Prep time:	5 minutes
Cook time:	15 minutes

TIP:
The hash may be topped with a well-cooked fried egg.

SERVE COUNTRY SKILLET HASH
WITH:

Hot Biscuits

This light meal will fill you up but not out. Plan to do the Quick Day menu (page 63)
the day after this menu is cooked, so the fish is at its best.

*S*nappy Halibut Skillet

½ tsp.	thyme
2 lb.	halibut *or* other firm white fish
1 tbsp.	olive oil
1	onion, chopped
1	clove garlic, minced
1 tbsp.	cornstarch
1 can	(14½ oz.) DEL MONTE® Stewed Tomatoes, No Salt Added
¼ cup	sliced green onions

■ Sprinkle thyme over both sides of fish. In large skillet, cook fish in hot oil over medium-high heat until fish flakes easily with fork. (Cool; cover and refrigerate about ½ lb. of fish for Quick Day, page 63.) Remove remaining fish to plate; keep warm.

■ In same skillet, cook onion and garlic until tender. Stir cornstarch into tomatoes; pour into skillet. Cook, stirring frequently, until thickened. Return fish to skillet; top with green onions. Heat through.

4 servings

Prep time: *5 minutes*
Cook time: *10 minutes*

DO-AHEAD NOTE:
Cook extra fish.

SERVE SNAPPY HALIBUT WITH:

Buttered Green Beans
French Bread

*This delicious soup takes advantage of already cooked fish (page 60).
Or use this fish in place of tuna in the Tarragon Tuna Pasta Salad (page 71).*

Fisherman's Soup

1	onion, chopped
1	clove garlic, crushed
1 tbsp.	vegetable oil
3 tbsp.	flour
2 cans	(14 oz. *each*) low-salt chicken broth
1 can	(14½ oz.) DEL MONTE® Whole New Potatoes, drained and chopped
1 can	(15¼ oz.) DEL MONTE Whole Kernel Corn, No Salt Added, undrained
½ lb.	cooked halibut

■ In large saucepan, cook onion and garlic in oil over medium heat until onion is tender. Stir in flour; cook 1 minute. Stir in broth; cook until thickened, stirring occasionally. Stir in potatoes and corn.

■ Discard skin and bones of fish (cooked on Cook Day, page 60); cut fish into bite-size pieces.

■ Just before serving, add fish to soup; heat through. Stir in chopped parsley or sliced green onions, if desired.

4 to 6 servings

Prep time:	*5 minutes*
Cook time:	*10 minutes*

SERVE FISHERMAN'S SOUP
WITH:

Hot Crusty French Rolls

This recipe makes a double batch of meat sauce. Serve some tonight and freeze the rest for later.

Zucchini Meat Sauce with Pasta

2 pkg.	(12 oz. *each*) shell macaroni *or* corkscrew pasta
2 lb.	ground beef
2	onions, chopped
2 cans	(26½ oz. *each*) DEL MONTE® Spaghetti Sauce With Garlic
1 can	(14½ oz.) DEL MONTE Fresh Cut Diced Tomatoes, undrained
2	small zucchini, thinly sliced

■ In 8-quart pot, cook pasta according to package directions; drain. (Rinse half of pasta in cold water; cover and refrigerate for Quick Day, page 67). Keep remaining pasta hot.

■ In 6-quart pot, brown meat over medium-high heat. Season with salt and pepper, if desired; drain. Add onions; cook until tender.

■ Stir in spaghetti sauce and tomatoes; cook 5 minutes, stirring occasionally. (Pour half of sauce into freezer container. Cool; cover and freeze for another meal.)

■ Add zucchini to remaining sauce; cover and cook over medium heat 7 to 10 minutes or until zucchini is tender. Serve sauce over hot pasta. Sprinkle with grated Parmesan cheese and garnish, if desired.

4 servings

Prep and cook time: *30 minutes*

TIPS:
• *If you don't have an 8-quart pot, cook the pasta in two batches.*
• *To freeze sauce, cool sauce slightly in an uncovered freezer container, and then tightly seal and freeze up to 6 months.*

DO-AHEAD NOTES:
Cook extra pasta.
Cook extra sauce to freeze.

> SERVE ZUCCHINI MEAT SAUCE WITH PASTA WITH:
>
> *Tossed Green Salad*
> *Herbed or Plain French Bread*

*An extra batch of pasta gets cooked ahead on Cook Day (page 64)
so this salad is ready in minutes.*

Caesar Shrimp Pasta Salad

1 can	(14½ oz.) **DEL MONTE®** **Pasta Style Chunky Tomatoes, drained**
1 lb.	**cooked tiny shrimp**
6 cups	**cooked shell macaroni** *or* **corkscrew pasta**
1	**small cucumber, diced**
1 cup	**Caesar dressing**
3	**green onions, sliced**

■ Drain tomatoes, reserving ⅓ cup liquid. In large bowl, combine reserved liquid with tomatoes, pasta (cooked on Cook Day, page 64) and remaining ingredients. Season with salt and pepper, if desired.

■ Cover and refrigerate until serving time. Garnish, if desired.

4 servings (2½ cups each)

Prep time: 10 minutes

SERVE CAESAR SHRIMP PASTA SALAD WITH:

Creamy Asparagus Potato Soup

1 can	(14½ oz.) DEL MONTE New Potatoes, drained
1 can	(15 oz.) DEL MONTE Asparagus Spears, drained
½ tsp.	thyme, crushed
⅛ tsp.	garlic powder
1 can	(14 oz.) chicken broth
1 cup	milk *or* half-and-half

Place potatoes, asparagus, thyme and garlic powder in food processor or blender (in batches if needed); process until smooth.

Pour into medium saucepan; add broth. Bring to a boil. Stir in milk; heat through. (Do not boil.) Season with salt and pepper, if desired. Serve hot or cold. Thin with additional milk or water, if desired.

4 servings

Crusty French Bread

Use some of the noodles tonight while they're hot, and save the rest to make
Tarragon Tuna Pasta Salad (page 71) later.

Cheeseburger Macaroni

2 cups	mostaccioli *or* elbow macaroni
1 lb.	ground beef
1	onion, chopped
1 can	(14½ oz.) DEL MONTE® Original *or* Italian Recipe Stewed Tomatoes
¼ cup	DEL MONTE Tomato Ketchup
1 cup	(4 oz.) shredded Cheddar cheese

■ Cook pasta according to package directions; drain. (Rinse 3 cups cooked pasta in cold water; cover and refrigerate for Quick Day, page 71).

■ In large skillet, brown meat with onion; drain. Season with salt and pepper, if desired. Stir in tomatoes, ketchup and remaining noodles; heat through.

■ Top with cheese. Garnish with sliced green onions, if desired.

4 servings

Prep time: *8 minutes*
Cook time: *15 minutes*

DO-AHEAD NOTE:
Cook extra pasta.

SERVE CHEESEBURGER MACARONI WITH:

Basil Carrots
1 can   (14½ oz.) DEL MONTE
Sliced Carrots, drained
1 tbsp. butter *or* margarine
½ tsp. basil, crushed

In small saucepan, heat carrots with butter and basil until heated through.
4 servings

Tarragon is a nice complement to the peas, carrots and tuna in this quick salad. Precooked noodles from Cook Day (page 68) make this salad extra convenient.

Tarragon Tuna Pasta Salad

½ cup	**mayonnaise**
½ tsp.	**tarragon *or* thyme, crushed**
3 cups	**cooked, chilled mostaccioli *or* elbow macaroni**
2	**stalks celery, sliced**
1 can	**(6⅛ oz.) solid white tuna in water, drained and flaked**
1 can	**(14½ oz.) DEL MONTE® Peas and Carrots, drained**

■ In large bowl, combine mayonnaise and tarragon. Add pasta (cooked on Cook Day, page 68), celery and tuna. Gently stir in peas and carrots.

■ Line large salad bowl with lettuce, if desired. Fill with salad.

4 servings

Prep time: *8 minutes*

HEALTHY HINT:
Use light mayonnaise instead of regular mayonnaise.

TIP:
Can be made ahead.

SERVE TARRAGON TUNA PASTA SALAD WITH:

Cream of Tomato Soup

Bread Sticks or Crackers

*When shaped into patties, this "meat loaf" bakes in about half the time.
Bake extra patties to make Layered Noodle Bake (page 75) as a quick second meal.*

*I*talian *Meat Loaf Patties*

2 pkg.	**(12 oz. *each*) extra wide noodles**
1 tbsp.	**butter *or* margarine, melted**
1 can	**(15 oz.) DEL MONTE® Italian *or* Original Sloppy Joe Sauce**
2 lb.	**ground beef *or* turkey**
1 cup	**dry bread crumbs**
2	**eggs, beaten**
1 tbsp.	**dried minced onion**

■ Preheat oven to 375°F.

■ In 8-quart pot, cook noodles according to package directions; drain. (Rinse half of noodles in cold water; cover and refrigerate for Quick Day, page 75.) Toss remaining noodles in butter; keep hot.

■ Set aside half of sauce to brush on patties. In large bowl, combine remaining sauce with remaining ingredients; mix with fork. On large, greased baking sheet, shape meat mixture into 8 (1-inch thick) oblong patties. Brush reserved sauce over patties.

■ Bake 20 minutes or until no longer pink in center. (Cool; cover and refrigerate half of cooked patties for Quick Day, page 75.) Serve remaining patties with hot, buttered noodles.

4 servings

Prep time: 5 minutes
Cook time: 20 minutes

DO-AHEAD NOTE:
Cook extra patties and noodles.

SERVE ITALIAN MEAT LOAF PATTIES WITH:

Peas and Corn

1 can	(15¼ oz.) DEL MONTE Whole Kernel Corn, drained
1 can	(8½ oz.) DEL MONTE Sweet Peas, drained
2 tsp.	butter or margarine
¼ tsp.	oregano
	Dash cayenne pepper

In small saucepan, cook vegetables with butter, oregano and cayenne over medium heat until heated through, stirring occasionally.

4 to 6 servings

Meat loaf patties (page 72) are transformed into a delicious lasagna-like dish when layered with lots of cheese, spaghetti sauce and noodles.

Layered Noodle Bake

1 can	**(26½ oz.) DEL MONTE® Spaghetti Sauce with Green Peppers and Mushrooms**
1 pkg.	**(12 oz.) extra wide noodles, cooked**
4	**Italian Meat Loaf Patties, cooked and cut bite-size**
1 pt.	**(16 oz.) low-fat ricotta *or* cottage cheese**
1 pkg.	**(8 oz.) shredded mozzarella cheese**

■ Preheat oven to 350°F.

■ Onto bottom of 13 x 9-inch baking pan, spread thin layer of sauce. Arrange half of noodles (cooked on Cook Day, page 72) over sauce; cover with half of remaining sauce.

■ Cover with meat (cooked on Cook Day, page 72), ricotta cheese and half of mozzarella cheese; top with layers of remaining noodles, sauce and mozzarella cheese.

■ Bake, uncovered, about 25 minutes or until heated through.

4 to 6 servings

Prep time: 5 minutes
Bake time: 25 minutes

HEALTHY HINT:
Substitute fat-free ricotta cheese and reduced-fat mozzarella cheese.

TIPS:
• *May be assembled ahead.*
• *Buy pre-shredded mozzarella cheese.*

SERVE LAYERED NOODLE BAKE WITH:

Quick Caesar Salad
6 cups torn romaine lettuce
Croutons
Bottled Caesar dressing

In large bowl, toss lettuce and croutons with dressing. Sprinkle with grated Parmesan cheese, if desired.

4 to 6 servings

While the pots are out, cook extra ravioli and sausage for another night's dinner
— the reward is Ravioli Soup (page 79) in just minutes.

*R*avioli with Tomatoes and Zucchini

3 pkg.	**(9 oz. *each*) fresh *or* frozen cheese ravioli *or* tortellini**
1½ lb.	**hot Italian sausage, crumbled**
2 cans	**(14½ oz. *each*) DEL MONTE® Fresh Cut Diced Tomatoes**
1	**medium zucchini, thinly sliced and quartered**
1 tsp.	**basil, crushed**
½ cup	**ricotta cheese *or* 2 tbsp. grated Parmesan cheese**

■ In 8-quart pot, cook pasta according to package directions; drain. Keep hot. (Rinse one third of cooked pasta in cold water; cover and refrigerate for Quick Day, page 79.)

■ Meanwhile, in 6-quart pot, brown sausage over medium-high heat until done; drain. (Remove half of sausage from pot. Cool; cover and refrigerate for Quick Day, page 79.)

■ To remaining sausage in pot, add tomatoes, zucchini and basil. Cook, uncovered, over medium-high heat about 8 minutes or until zucchini is just tender-crisp, stirring occasionally. Season with pepper, if desired.

■ Spoon sauce over hot pasta. Top with ricotta cheese.

4 servings

Prep and cook time: 20 minutes

DO-AHEAD NOTE:
Cook extra sausage and ravioli.

SERVE RAVIOLI WITH TOMATOES AND ZUCCHINI WITH:

Romaine and Beet Salad
6 cups chopped romaine lettuce
1 can   (8¼ oz.) DEL MONTE
   Sliced Beets, drained
   Blue cheese, crumbled
   Oil and vinegar dressing
In large bowl, toss lettuce, beets and cheese with dressing.
4 to 6 servings

Sesame Bread Sticks or French Bread

Making canned soups isn't much easier than preparing this hearty soup. Nor are canned soups half as tasty! The sausage and ravioli are cooked with a previous meal (page 76) for good, fast food. Now.

Ravioli Soup

¾ lb.	**hot Italian sausage, crumbled and cooked**
1 can	**(14½ oz.) DEL MONTE® Italian Recipe Stewed Tomatoes**
1 can	**(14 oz.) beef broth**
1 pkg.	**(9 oz.) fresh *or* frozen cheese ravioli *or* tortellini, cooked and drained**
1 can	**(14½ oz.) DEL MONTE Italian Green Beans, drained**
2	**green onions, sliced**

■ In 5-quart pot, combine sausage (cooked on Cook Day, page 76), tomatoes, broth and 1¾ cups water; bring to boil over high heat.

■ Reduce heat to low; stir in ravioli (cooked on Cook Day, page 76), beans and onions. Gently cook until ravioli are heated through.

■ Season with pepper and sprinkle with grated Parmesan cheese, if desired.

4 servings (about 2½ cups each)

Prep and cook time: 15 minutes

TIPS:
• *Bake the bread while the soup cooks.*
• *Spoon any leftover soup into a shallow bowl or dish for quick, safe cooling.*

SERVE RAVIOLI SOUP WITH:

Garlic Bread
½ stick (¼ cup) butter or margarine, softened
⅛ tsp. garlic powder
½ loaf French bread, sliced in half lengthwise

In small bowl, combine butter and garlic powder. Spread over cut sides of French bread. Bake at 450°F until lightly browned, about 4 minutes.

4 servings

Bruschetta

1 can	(14½ oz.) DEL MONTE® Italian Recipe Stewed Tomatoes
1 to 2	cloves garlic, crushed
2 tbsp.	chopped fresh basil *or* ½ tsp. dried basil
½ loaf	baguette French bread, cut into ½-inch slices
1 tbsp.	olive oil

■ Preheat broiler. Drain tomatoes reserving liquid. In small saucepan, boil reserved liquid with garlic, 5 to 6 minutes, stirring occasionally. Remove from heat.

■ Chop tomatoes; combine with garlic mixture and basil. Brush bread with oil. Broil until golden. Top with tomato mixture; serve immediately.

6 servings

Caponata

1 lb.	eggplant, cut into ⅜-inch cubes
3	large cloves garlic, minced
¼ cup	olive oil
1 can	(14¼ oz.) DEL MONTE Italian Recipe Stewed Tomatoes
1	green pepper, finely chopped
1 can	(2¼ oz.) chopped ripe olives
2 tbsp.	lemon juice
1 tsp.	basil, crushed
1	(12-inch) prepared, pre-baked pizza crust, cut into slices or 1 loaf baguette French bread, cut into ¼-inch slices

■ In skillet, cook eggplant and garlic in oil over medium heat 5 minutes. Season with salt and pepper, if desired. Stir in remaining ingredients, except pizza crust.

■ Cook, uncovered, 10 minutes or until thick. Chill. Serve with slices of pizza crust.

Approximately 4½ cups

Caponata (top), Bruschetta

Cocktail Kabobs (left), Shrimp and Chili Sauce Over Cream Cheese

*S*hrimp and Chili Sauce Over Cream Cheese

1 pkg.	(8 oz.) cream cheese *or* Neufchatel cheese, softened
	Lettuce leaves (optional)
½ cup	DEL MONTE® Chili Sauce *or* Seafood Cocktail Sauce
¼ lb.	cooked tiny shrimp
	Assorted crackers

■ Place cream cheese on plate over lettuce leaves, if desired.

■ Just before serving, spoon sauce and shrimp over cheese. Serve with crackers.

6 to 8 servings

HELPFUL HINT:
For a festive touch, shape the cheese into a log, ball or oval and then roll it in finely chopped parsley.

Cocktail Kabobs

1 can	**(20 oz.) DEL MONTE® Pineapple Chunks In Its Own Juice, drained**
1 can	**(11 oz.) DEL MONTE Mandarin Oranges, drained**
1 lb.	**cooked ham, cut into ¾-inch cubes**
	Mustard Dressing (see recipe below)

■ Thread pineapple chunks, orange sections and ham cubes alternately on skewers. Serve with dressing.

Approximately 24 appetizers

Mustard Dressing

¾ cup	**salad oil**
3 tbsp.	**red wine vinegar**
2 tbsp.	**Dijon mustard**
½ tsp.	**salt**
¼ tsp.	**freshly ground pepper**

■ Place ingredients in blender container. Cover and run on medium until smooth.

Approximately 1¼ cups

1. Thread pineapple chunks, ham cubes and orange sections on skewers.

2. Place oil, vinegar, mustard, salt and pepper in blender container.

3. Serve kabobs with dressing.

Cheesy Asparagus Spread

1 can	(15 oz.) DEL MONTE® Tender Green Asparagus Spears, drained and chopped
½ cup	grated Parmesan cheese
⅓ cup	light *or* regular mayonnaise
⅓ cup	chopped green onion
⅛ tsp.	garlic powder

■ Combine all ingredients in 1-quart baking dish. Smooth top. Clean sides of dish. Bake at 375°F, 30 minutes or until hot.

■ Garnish with additional chopped green onion, if desired. Serve immediately with sliced French bread or crackers.

8 servings

Microwave Directions: Combine all ingredients in 1-quart microwavable dish. Cook, uncovered, on HIGH 8 to 10 minutes or until hot; stir and smooth halfway through.

Garnish with additional chopped green onion, if desired. Serve immediately with sliced French bread or crackers.

Creamy Vegetable Dip

1 can	(13½ oz.) DEL MONTE Chopped Spinach
2 cups	light sour cream
1 pkg.	(1.4 oz.) dry vegetable soup mix
¼ cup	light mayonnaise
1 can	(8 oz.) water chestnuts, drained and chopped

■ Drain spinach well reserving 2 tablespoons liquid. Combine reserved liquid, sour cream, soup mix and mayonnaise. Stir in spinach and water chestnuts.

■ Refrigerate several hours or overnight to blend flavors. Serve with vegetables, bread or crackers.

4 cups

Cheesy Asparagus Spread (left), Neptune Crab Spread (center), Creamy Vegetable Dip

Neptune Crab Spread

8 oz.	cream cheese, softened
¼ cup	DEL MONTE® Seafood Cocktail Sauce
¼ cup	sour cream
1 tbsp.	lemon juice
½ tsp.	dill weed
1 tbsp.	chopped green onion
6 oz.	imitation crab, flaked*

■ In bowl, combine cream cheese, cocktail sauce, sour cream, lemon juice and dill weed; beat until smooth. Stir in onion and crab.

■ Serve with crackers, sliced bread or vegetables.

1½ cups

* Variation:
6 oz. chopped cooked shrimp or canned crab may be used.

Dilly Carrot Dip

1 can	(14½ oz.) DEL MONTE® Sliced Carrots, drained
½ cup	sour cream
1 tbsp.	DEL MONTE Tomato Ketchup
¼ tsp.	crushed dill weed
¼ tsp.	garlic powder
¼ tsp.	onion powder
⅛ tsp.	ground pepper

■ Place ingredients in food processor. Cover and process with metal blade until smooth.

■ Serve with assorted crackers and vegetable dippers. Or cover and store in refrigerator until ready to use. Stir before using.

Makes 1½ cups

Green Bean Croustades

12	thin slices white bread
12	thin slices wheat bread
1 tbsp.	butter *or* margarine, melted
½ cup	grated Gruyère cheese
1 can	(14½ oz.) DEL MONTE Cut Green Beans, drained
¼ cup	whipping cream
⅛ tsp.	chili powder
2 tbsp.	chopped pimiento
1 tbsp.	sesame seeds, toasted

■ Cut bread into 2½-inch rounds. Grease 2-inch muffin cups with melted butter.

■ Press bread into muffin cups. Bake at 350°F, 10 minutes or until golden.

■ Divide cheese evenly among cups. Arrange beans over cheese. Mix cream and chili powder; spoon over beans. Top with pimiento and sesame seeds.

■ Bake at 350°F, 10 minutes; serve warm.

Makes 2 dozen

Zucchini Chicken Soup

½ cup	chopped onion
½ cup	chopped carrot
1	clove garlic, minced
1 tbsp.	butter or margarine
1 cup	diced cooked chicken
1 can	(14½ oz.) DEL MONTE® Zucchini with Italian-Style Tomato Sauce
1 can	(14 oz.) chicken broth

■ Sauté onion, carrot and garlic in butter, about 5 minutes.

■ Add remaining ingredients. Heat through and serve.

Makes 5 cups

Ginger Carrot Soup (top), Tortilla Soup

Ginger Carrot Soup

1	medium onion, diced
2 tbsp.	safflower oil
1	medium potato, diced
1 can	(14 oz.) low-salt chicken broth
2 tsp.	grated ginger root
1 can	(14½ oz.) DEL MONTE® Sliced Carrots
½ cup	lowfat milk *or* whole milk
	Dash white pepper

■ Cook onion in oil until soft. Add potato, chicken broth, ginger and liquid from carrots. Bring to boil. Reduce heat; cover and simmer 20 minutes.

■ Pour into blender or food processor container. Add carrots; cover and run on high until smooth and well blended.

■ Stir in milk and pepper. Heat through; *do not boil.* Serve hot or cold.

4 to 6 servings

HELPFUL HINT:
Make ahead. Cover and refrigerate until ready to serve. Stir in water if thinner consistency is desired.

Tortilla Soup

1 can	(14½ oz.) DEL MONTE Mexican Recipe Stewed Tomatoes, coarsely chopped
2 cans	(14 oz. *each*) low-salt chicken broth
1	medium onion, chopped
1	clove garlic, crushed
¼ tsp.	ground cumin
½ lb.	ground turkey *or* beef
1½ cups	crushed tortilla chips
	Cilantro

■ In large pot, combine tomatoes, broth, onion, garlic and cumin; simmer 5 minutes. Break meat into bite-size chunks; add to soup. Simmer until cooked, about 8 minutes.

■ Top individual servings with tortilla chips and cilantro. Serve with shredded Monterey Jack cheese, if desired.

6 servings (1 cup each)

Gazpacho

1 can	(14½ oz.) DEL MONTE® Original Recipe Stewed Tomatoes, puréed
1 can	(15 oz.) *or* 2 cans (8 oz. *each*) DEL MONTE Tomato Sauce
¾ cup	finely chopped celery
¾ cup	finely chopped cucumber
½ cup	finely chopped onion
½ cup	water
¼ cup	finely chopped green bell pepper
¼ cup	red wine vinegar
2 tbsp.	chopped parsley
2 tbsp.	olive oil
1 tsp.	Worcestershire sauce
¼ tsp.	pepper
	Dash garlic powder

■ Combine all ingredients; mix well. Chill several hours.

■ Serve with dollop of sour cream or plain yogurt, if desired.

6 to 8 servings

Gazpacho

Autumn Beef Vegetable Soup

1 lb.	lean ground beef
½ cup	chopped onion
2 cans	(14½ oz. *each*) DEL MONTE® Italian Recipe Stewed Tomatoes
2 cans	(14 oz. *each*) beef broth
1 can	(14½ oz.) DEL MONTE Mixed Vegetables
½ cup	uncooked medium egg noodles
½ tsp.	oregano

■ In large pot, brown meat with onion. Cook until onion is tender; drain. Add salt and pepper to taste, if desired.

■ Stir in remaining ingredients. Bring to boil; reduce heat. Cover and simmer 15 minutes or until noodles are tender.

8 servings (1 cup each)

Chicken Curry Bombay

1	medium onion, cut in wedges
2	cloves garlic, minced
2 tsp.	curry powder
1 tbsp.	olive oil
2	half boneless chicken breasts, skinned and sliced ¼-inch wide
1 can	(14¼ oz.) DEL MONTE® Original Recipe Stewed Tomatoes
⅓ cup	DEL MONTE Seedless Raisins
1 can	(14½ oz.) DEL MONTE Whole New Potatoes, drained and cut in chunks
1 can	(14½ oz.) DEL MONTE Cut Green Beans, drained

■ In skillet, cook onion, garlic and curry in oil until tender, stirring occasionally.

■ Stir in chicken, tomatoes and raisins; bring to boil. Cover and simmer 8 minutes. Add potatoes and green beans.

■ Cook, uncovered, 5 minutes, stirring occasionally. Season to taste with salt and pepper, if desired.

4 servings

Marsala Apricot Chicken

1 can	(15 oz.) DEL MONTE® Lite Apricot Halves
1 tbsp.	orange juice concentrate
⅓ cup	marsala wine
4	half chicken breasts, skinned and boned
2 tbsp.	chopped parsley
½ tsp.	paprika
½ tsp.	salt
¼ tsp.	rosemary, crushed
1	clove garlic, minced
1 tbsp.	oil

■ Reserve 4 to 8 apricot halves for garnish. Pour remaining apricots with liquid and orange juice concentrate into blender container.

■ Cover and blend until smooth; pour into small saucepan. Bring to boil. Cook, uncovered until reduced to ¾ cup, about 7 to 10 minutes. Add marsala; cook 1 minute. Keep warm.

■ Lightly pound each chicken breast. Combine parsley, paprika, salt and rosemary. Pat onto both sides of each breast.

■ Sauté garlic in oil. Add chicken; cook 4 to 5 minutes on each side or until done.

■ Garnish each serving with reserved apricots and serve with sauce.

4 servings

Fiesta Chicken Chili

*F*iesta Chicken Chili

1	**half boneless chicken breast, skinned**
1	**onion, chopped**
2	**cloves garlic, crushed**
1 tbsp.	**oil**
1 can	**(14¼ oz.) DEL MONTE® Chili Style Chunky Tomatoes**
1 can	**(15 oz.) pinto beans, drained**
1 can	**(4 oz.) diced green chiles**

■ Cut chicken into thin strips.

■ In large saucepan, cook chicken, onion and garlic in oil; drain. Add tomatoes, beans and chiles. Simmer 10 minutes.

■ Garnish with avocado and chopped cilantro, if desired.

4 servings

Variation:
For a zesty bean chili, omit chicken.

*S*anta Fe Chicken

2½ lb.	**chicken pieces, skinned (breasts, thighs and legs)**
1 tbsp.	**oil**
½ tsp.	**cumin**
1	**clove garlic, crushed**
1 can	**(8 oz.) DEL MONTE Tomato Sauce**
1 can	**(14½ oz.) DEL MONTE Mexican Recipe Stewed Tomatoes**
1 can	**(4 oz.) diced green chiles**
2	**zucchini, sliced**

■ In large skillet, brown chicken in oil, 10 to 15 minutes; drain. Add salt and pepper to taste, if desired.

■ Stir cumin and garlic into tomato sauce; pour over chicken. Add remaining ingredients. Cover and simmer 10 minutes.

■ Uncover and cook on high 10 minutes or until chicken is done.

■ Serve with hot cooked rice, if desired.

4 to 6 servings

Chicken Athena

1 lb.	boneless chicken, skinned and cut into cubes
1 tbsp.	olive oil
1	onion, cut into chunks
1 can	(14½ oz.) DEL MONTE® Original Recipe Stewed Tomatoes
1 jar	(6 oz.) marinated artichoke hearts
¼ tsp.	rosemary, crushed
⅓ cup	crumbled feta cheese (optional)

■ In skillet, brown chicken in oil over medium-high heat; add onion and cook 2 minutes.

■ Stir in tomatoes, marinade from artichokes and rosemary; cook over medium heat 10 to 15 minutes or until thickened, stirring frequently. Stir in artichoke hearts; heat through.

■ Top with cheese. Garnish with chopped parsley, if desired.

4 to 6 servings

Variation:
Substitute fresh turkey for chicken.

Sicilian Skillet Chicken

4	half boneless chicken breasts, skinned
6 tbsp.	grated Parmesan cheese
3 tbsp.	flour
2 tbsp.	olive oil
1 cup	sliced mushrooms
½	onion, finely chopped
½ tsp.	rosemary, crushed
1 can	(14½ oz.) DEL MONTE Italian Recipe Stewed Tomatoes

■ Flatten chicken slightly. Coat with 4 tablespoons cheese and then flour. Season with salt and pepper, if desired.

■ Preheat oil in skillet over medium-high heat. Cook chicken until done, turning once. Remove to serving dish; keep warm.

■ In same skillet, cook mushrooms, onion and rosemary until soft. Add tomatoes; cook, uncovered, over medium-high heat until thickened.

■ Spoon over chicken; top with remaining cheese. Serve over rice, and garnish with chopped parsley, if desired.

4 servings

Chicken Athena

*S*outhwestern Corn and Sausage Sauté

½ lb.	spicy sausage links
2	half chicken breasts, boned and skinned
1	medium green pepper, cut into strips
1 tbsp.	oil
⅔ cup	DEL MONTE® Thick & Chunky Salsa, Mild or Medium
1 can	(15¼ oz.) DEL MONTE Whole Kernel Golden Sweet Corn, drained
⅓ cup	whipping cream

■ Cut sausage in ¼-inch slices. Cut chicken in 1 x 2-inch strips.

■ In 10-inch skillet, brown sausage over medium-high heat, turning once. Remove from pan.

■ Add chicken to pan and brown both sides. Remove from pan.

■ Cook peppers in oil over medium-high heat 2 minutes.

■ Return sausage and chicken to pan. Stir in salsa; simmer, uncovered, 3 minutes.

■ Reduce heat; add vegetables and cream. Heat through. Garnish with chopped cilantro, if desired. Serve immediately.

4 servings

Chicken Pesto Mozzarella

6 to 8 oz. corkscrew pasta	
4	**half boneless chicken breasts, skinned**
1 tbsp.	**olive oil**
1 can	**(14½ oz.) DEL MONTE® Pasta Style Chunky Tomatoes**
½	**onion, chopped**
⅓ cup	**sliced ripe olives**
4 tsp.	**pesto sauce***
¼ cup	**shredded skim milk mozzarella cheese**

■ Cook pasta according to package directions; drain. Season chicken with salt and pepper, if desired.

■ In skillet, brown chicken in oil over medium-high heat. Add tomatoes, onion and olives; bring to boil. Cover and cook 8 minutes over medium heat. Remove cover; cook over medium-high heat about 8 minutes until chicken is done.

■ Spread 1 teaspoon pesto over each breast; top with cheese. Cover and cook until cheese melts. Serve over pasta.

4 servings

*HELPFUL HINT:
Available frozen or refrigerated at supermarket.

Coq au Vin

4	thin slices bacon, cut into ½-inch pieces
6	chicken thighs, skinned
¾ tsp.	thyme, crushed
1	large onion, coarsely chopped
4	cloves garlic, minced
½ lb.	small red potatoes, quartered
10	mushrooms, quartered
1 can	(14½ oz.) DEL MONTE® Italian Recipe Stewed Tomatoes
1½ cups	dry red wine

■ In 4-quart heavy pot, cook bacon until just starting to brown.

■ Sprinkle chicken with thyme; season with salt and pepper, if desired. Add chicken to pan; brown over medium-high heat. Add onion and garlic. Cook 2 minutes; drain.

■ Add potatoes, mushrooms, tomatoes and wine. Cook, uncovered, over medium-high heat about 25 minutes or until potatoes are tender and sauce thickens, stirring occasionally.

■ Garnish with chopped parsley, if desired.

4 to 6 servings

Black Bean Garnachas

Peachy Honey Mustard Chicken

1 can	(15 oz.) DEL MONTE® Lite Sliced Yellow Cling Peaches
2½ lb.	broiler-fryer chicken, cut up
1 tbsp.	vegetable oil
3 tbsp.	Dijon mustard
1 tbsp.	honey
¼ cup	sliced green onion

■ Drain peaches reserving liquid. Skin chicken, if desired.

■ Heat oil in 12-inch skillet. Add chicken, brown on both sides over high heat; drain.

■ Blend reserved peach liquid with mustard and honey. Pour over chicken, cover, reduce heat and simmer 10 minutes or until cooked through.

■ Remove chicken to serving plate. Add peaches and green onions.

■ Boil over high heat to thicken slightly, about 5 minutes. Spoon over chicken.

4 servings

Black Bean Garnachas

1 can	(14½ oz.) DEL MONTE® Mexican Recipe Stewed Tomatoes
1 can	(15 oz.) black or pinto beans, drained
2	cloves garlic, minced
1 tsp	minced jalapeño chile (optional)
½ tsp.	ground cumin
1 cup	cubed grilled chicken
4	flour tortillas
½ cup	shredded sharp Cheddar cheese

■ Drain tomatoes reserving liquid. Chop tomatoes.

■ In skillet, combine tomatoes, reserved liquid, beans, garlic, jalapeño and cumin. Cook over medium-high heat, 5 to 7 minutes or until thickened, stirring occasionally. Season with salt and pepper, if desired. Add chicken.

■ Arrange tortillas in a single layer on grill over medium coals.

■ Spread about ¼ cup chicken mixture over tortilla. Top with cheese. Repeat with remaining tortillas.

■ Cook about 3 minutes or until bottom of tortilla browns and cheese melts.

■ Garnish with shredded lettuce and diced avocado, if desired.

4 servings

Variation:
Prepare chicken mixture as directed above. Place a tortilla in dry skillet over medium heat. Spread with about ¼ cup chicken mixture; top with 2 tablespoons cheese. Cook about 3 minutes or until bottom of tortilla browns and cheese melts.

Curried Tomato Apple Chicken

4	**half boneless chicken breasts, skinned**
1 can	**(14½ oz.) DEL MONTE® Original Recipe Stewed Tomatoes**
½ cup	**DEL MONTE Seedless Raisins**
½ cup	**sliced green onions, in 1-inch pieces**
2 tsp.	**curry powder**
1	**green apple, thinly sliced**
	Hot cooked couscous, bulgur *or* rice

■ Cut chicken into 1-inch pieces.

■ In large skillet, combine chicken, tomatoes, raisins and curry. Cook over medium heat, stirring frequently, about 10 minutes or until chicken is tender.

■ Add onions and apple. Bring to boil and reduce heat. Simmer, uncovered, about 10 minutes or until sauce thickens.

■ Serve over hot cooked couscous, bulgur or rice.

4 servings

Turkey Breast with Apricot-Bourbon Sauce

Turkey Encore

6 oz.	elbow macaroni
¼ cup	butter *or* margarine
1 cup	sliced onion
1 cup	chopped celery
½ cup	chopped green bell pepper
⅓ cup	flour
1 can	(14 oz.) chicken broth
2 cans	(14½ oz. *each*) DEL MONTE® Original Recipe Stewed Tomatoes
4 cups	cubed cooked turkey
1½ cups	shredded Cheddar cheese
1½ tsp.	basil
¼ tsp.	pepper

■ In large saucepan, cook macaroni in boiling water until almost tender; drain.

■ Melt butter in large skillet. Add onion, celery and green pepper; cook until tender.

■ Stir in flour; cook 1 to 2 minutes. Add broth. Cook, stirring constantly, until thickened. Stir in tomatoes, turkey, ¾ cup cheese, basil and pepper.

■ Pour into greased 2½-quart casserole. Cover and bake at 350°F, 20 minutes. Uncover; bake 25 minutes longer. Top with remaining cheese. Cover and let stand 3 to 4 minutes.

6 to 8 servings

*T*urkey Breast with Apricot-Bourbon Sauce

2 cans	(15¼ oz. *each*) DEL MONTE® Apricot Halves
1 cup	orange juice
½ cup	bourbon
1 tsp.	salt
½ tsp.	fines herbes
¼ tsp.	pepper
⅛ tsp.	garlic powder
2	half turkey breasts (3 to 4 lb. *each*)
1 tbsp.	cornstarch
2 tbsp.	butter *or* margarine, cut up
	Parsley sprigs

■ Drain fruit reserving syrup; set fruit aside. Combine reserved syrup, orange juice, bourbon, salt, fines herbes, pepper and garlic powder. Add meat.

■ Cover and marinate at room temperature, 1 hour or overnight in refrigerator. Remove meat from marinade; drain well, reserving marinade. Cover and bake on roasting rack at 350°F, 2 to 3 hours or until done, basting occasionally with reserved marinade.

■ Let stand 20 minutes before slicing.

■ Drain pan juices into saucepan; add remaining marinade. Bring to boil; cook until reduced by half, about 15 minutes.

■ Purée half the apricots; stir into reduced sauce. Dissolve cornstarch in 1 tablespoon cold water; add to sauce, stirring constantly until thickened and translucent. Remove from heat.

■ Add butter; whisk until smooth. Spoon some sauce over turkey; garnish with reserved apricot halves and parsley. Serve with remaining sauce.

10 servings (2½ cups sauce)

Cajun Cornish Hens

4 oz.	hot smoked sausage, chopped
½ cup	long-grain white rice
1 can	(14½ oz.) DEL MONTE® Cajun Recipe Stewed Tomatoes
½ cup	sliced green onion
¼ cup	chopped green pepper
1	clove garlic, minced
¼ tsp.	thyme
4	medium (approximately 1¼ lb. *each*) Rock Cornish hens, thawed
1 tbsp.	butter, melted

■ Brown sausage in saucepan. Stir in rice; cook 2 minutes. Add tomatoes, onion, pepper, garlic and thyme. Bring to boil. Cover and simmer 20 minutes (rice will be firm).

■ Remove giblet package from hens and set aside for another use. Stuff hens with rice mixture. Tie legs together with string. Place breast side up on rack in shallow pan. Brush with butter.

■ Bake at 375°F, 1 hour or until done. Remove string from legs and serve.

4 servings

1. Stuff hens with rice mixture.

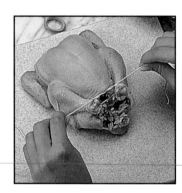

2. Tie legs together with string.

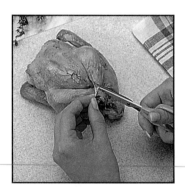

3. Trim string and place hens breast side up on rack in baking pan.

Beef Quesadillas with Tomatoes and Cilantro

1 can	(14½ oz.) DEL MONTE® Mexican Recipe Stewed Tomatoes
2 tsp.	minced jalapeño chile
1 cup	chopped, cooked roast beef *or* steak
1 can	(8 oz.) low-salt kidney beans, drained
⅓ cup	chopped cilantro
6	flour tortillas
⅔ cup	shredded Monterey Jack cheese

■ In skillet, combine tomatoes and jalapeño. Cook, uncovered, over medium-high heat 8 minutes or until thickened, stirring occasionally.

■ Stir in beef, beans and cilantro; heat through.

■ Place tortilla in preheated dry skillet over medium-low heat. Immediately spread about ⅓ cup meat mixture over half of tortilla; top with cheese. Fold other half of tortilla over meat to enclose.

■ Cook, uncovered, a minute or two until bottom of tortilla browns slightly. Turn over and cook until other side browns.

6 quesadillas

Variation:
Substitute 1 cup cooked shredded chicken for beef.

1. *Jalapeños contain oils that can burn eyes, lips and skin. Handle carefully.*

2. *Place tortilla in preheated skillet and spoon ⅓ cup meat mixture over one half.*

3. *Fold half of tortilla over meat to cover and enclose.*

Beef Quesadillas with Tomatoes and Cilantro

Zucchini Beef Scramble

1 lb.	ground beef
2 tbsp.	chopped green onion
1 can	(14½ oz.) DEL MONTE® Zucchini With Italian Style Tomato Sauce
1/2 tsp.	crushed oregano
	Salt and pepper to taste
1 cup	cubed Monterey Jack *or* Cheddar cheese

■ In 10-inch skillet, brown meat. Drain. Stir in onion, zucchini, oregano, salt and pepper. Dot with cheese.

■ Cover and simmer 10 to 15 minutes or until cheese melts. Serve with garlic bread, if desired.

4 to 6 servings

Apricot Beef Stir-Fry

1 lb.	flank steak
2 tbsp.	oil
½ tsp.	minced ginger root
1	clove garlic, crushed
1 can	(15 oz.) DEL MONTE® Lite Apricot Halves
¾ cup	beef broth
2 tbsp.	soy sauce
2 tbsp.	cornstarch
½ cup	sliced onion
3 cups	broccoli florets
	Hot cooked rice

■ Cut meat crosswise into thick strips.

■ Heat 1 tablespoon oil in wok or large skillet. Add ginger and garlic; stir-fry 1 minute. Add meat; stir-fry just until pink is gone. Remove meat; set aside.

■ Drain apricots reserving ½ cup liquid. Combine reserved liquid, broth, soy sauce and cornstarch; stir to dissolve cornstarch.

■ Heat remaining tablespoon oil in wok. Add onion and broccoli; stir-fry until tender-crisp. Add soy sauce mixture. Cook, stirring constantly, until thickened and translucent.

■ Add meat and apricots; heat through. Serve over rice.

4 to 6 servings

HELPFUL HINT:
Place meat in freezer 1 to 2 hours prior to cutting for easier slicing.

Grilled Beef Steak Ranchero

1 can	(14½ oz.) DEL MONTE® Mexican Recipe Stewed Tomatoes
1	clove garlic, minced
3 tbsp.	fresh lime juice
1 tsp.	hot pepper sauce
¾ lb.	lean round steak
1 can	(8½ oz.) low-salt kidney *or* garbanzo beans
⅓ cup	sliced green onions
2 tbsp.	chopped cilantro *or* parsley

■ Drain tomatoes reserving juice. Combine reserved juice, garlic, lime juice and pepper sauce. Pour half over meat; marinate ½ hour.

■ Coarsely chop tomatoes; combine with remaining marinade, beans, onions and cilantro. Remove meat; season to taste with salt and pepper, if desired.

■ Cook over hot coals 4 minutes per side or until done as desired.

■ Slice thin; top with salsa. Garnish with lime wedges, if desired.

4 servings (2 cups salsa)

Variation:
Top sirloin may be substituted.

HELPFUL HINT:
If meat marinates more than ½ hour, be sure to cover and refrigerate.

French Country Beef Stew

1½ lb.	stew beef, cut in 1-inch cubes
¼ cup	flour
2 tbsp.	oil
2 cans	(14½ oz. *each*) DEL MONTE® Original Recipe Stewed Tomatoes
1 can	(14 oz.) beef broth
4	medium carrots, pared, cut in 1-inch chunks
2	medium potatoes, pared, cut in 1-inch chunks
¾ tsp.	thyme
2 tbsp.	Dijon mustard (optional)

■ Combine meat and flour in plastic bag; toss to coat evenly.

■ In 6-quart pot, brown meat in oil. Season with salt and pepper, if desired.

■ Add remaining ingredients, except mustard. Bring to boil; reduce heat. Cover and simmer 1 hour or until beef is tender. Blend in mustard.

■ Garnish with chopped parsley and serve with warm crusty French bread, if desired.

6 to 8 servings

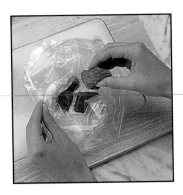

1. Cut stew beef into 1-inch cubes. Place cubes in plastic bag with flour.

2. Shake bag to thoroughly coat meat with flour. Make sure meat is evenly coated.

3. Brown meat in oil. This helps to seal in natural juices.

Vermont Veal Roast

1	**(3 lb.) rolled shoulder of veal**
1 tbsp.	**oil**
2	**cloves garlic, minced**
1 tsp.	**rosemary, crushed**
¼ tsp.	**pepper**
½ cup	**chopped shallot *or* onion**
1 can	**(14 oz.) chicken broth**
1 can	**(14½ oz.) DEL MONTE® Original Recipe Stewed Tomatoes**
1	**bay leaf**

■ Rub meat on all sides with oil, garlic, rosemary and pepper. Place meat in roasting pan. Sprinkle shallots around meat. Add remaining ingredients.

■ Roast, uncovered, at 375°F, 1½ hours, basting occasionally, until meat is tender. Remove meat; keep warm.

■ Skim fat from pan juices; thicken with 2 tablespoons flour dissolved with 3 tablespoons water. Serve with steamed, small red potatoes, if desired.

6 servings

Variation:
A pork roast may be substituted for the veal roast. Cook at 325°F, 2 to 2½ hours or until internal temperature reaches 170°F.

Arizona Beef Stew

1 lb.	**sirloin steak, thinly sliced, crosswise**
1 tbsp.	**oil**
½	**onion, chopped**
2 tsp.	**chili powder**
1 can	**(15 oz.) black or pinto beans**
1 can	**(14½ oz.) DEL MONTE® Mexican Recipe Stewed Tomatoes**
1 tsp.	**minced jalapeño chile**
1	**medium green bell pepper, cut in strips**

■ In skillet, brown meat in oil with onion and chili powder over medium-high heat. Add salt and pepper to taste.

■ Stir in beans, tomatoes and jalapeño. Cover and cook over medium heat 15 minutes, stirring occasionally.

■ Add green pepper. Cook, uncovered, 5 minutes or until thickened and meat is tender, stirring occasionally.

■ Serve with warm tortillas, lime wedges and sour cream, if desired.

4 to 6 servings

HELPFUL HINT:
After cutting raw meat, thoroughly clean cutting board in hot, soapy water.

Skillet Beef and Corn

½ lb.	sirloin steak, thinly sliced
1	medium onion, chopped
½ tsp.	thyme, crushed
1 tbsp.	olive oil
½ cup	dry red wine
1 can	(14½ oz.) DEL MONTE® Stewed Tomatoes (No Salt Added)
1 can	(15¼ oz.) DEL MONTE Whole Kernel Golden Sweet Corn (No Salt Added), drained
1 cup	cooked rice

■ In skillet, brown meat, onion and thyme in oil. Season with pepper, if desired.

■ Stir in wine; bring to boil. Simmer, uncovered, over medium heat, about 7 minutes or until liquid is evaporated. Add tomatoes; reduce heat. Cover and cook 15 minutes or until meat is tender.

■ Uncover and cook 5 minutes more. Add corn and rice; heat through. Garnish with sliced green onions, if desired.

4 servings

Japantown Flank Steak

½ cup	**DEL MONTE® Pineapple Juice**
½ cup	**soy sauce**
¼ tsp.	**garlic salt**
1¼ lb.	**flank steak**
2	**oranges, cut into thick slices**

■ Combine pineapple juice, soy sauce and garlic salt. Score meat on each side; marinate one hour or longer in pineapple-soy mixture; turn occasionally. (Marinade that has come in contact with raw meat must be boiled a few minutes before serving.)

■ Broil 8 to 10 minutes on each side or until cooked as desired, basting with marinade.

■ Garnish with orange or pineapple slices. Thinly slice meat across the grain to serve.

4 servings

Mardi Gras Beef Broil

½ lb.	steak, 1-inch thick
½ tsp.	garlic powder
½	onion, cut in chunks
½	small green bell pepper, cut in strips
¼ tsp.	thyme, crushed
1 tbsp.	oil
1 can	(8 oz.) DEL MONTE® Original Recipe Stewed Tomatoes
1 tsp.	cornstarch

■ Sprinkle meat with ¼ teaspoon garlic powder. Broil 5 inches from heat, 6 to 8 minutes for medium-rare, or until cooked as desired, turning once.

■ In skillet, cook onion, green bell pepper, thyme and remaining garlic powder in oil until vegetables are tender-crisp.

■ Drain tomatoes reserving juice; combine juice and cornstarch. Add to vegetables; cook, stirring constantly, until thickened. Add tomatoes; heat through. Add salt and pepper to taste.

■ Thinly slice meat; top with vegetables.

2 servings

Variation:
Substitute DEL MONTE Mexican Recipe Stewed Tomatoes and ¼ teaspoon oregano instead of thyme.

Quick Tomato Beef

1 lb.	lean ground beef
1 can	(14½ oz.) DEL MONTE Original Recipe Stewed Tomatoes
1	medium onion, cut in chunks
½	green bell pepper, cut in strips
⅛ tsp.	cayenne pepper
1 can	(14½ oz.) DEL MONTE Sliced New Potatoes, drained
1 cup	shredded Monterey Jack or Cheddar cheese

■ In skillet, brown meat; drain. Drain tomatoes; add liquid to skillet. Add onion, green pepper and cayenne.

■ Cook over high heat 5 to 8 minutes or until slightly thickened, stirring often.

■ Stir in tomatoes and potatoes; heat through. Top with cheese; heat until melted.

4 servings

Hungarian Pork Paprika

2 tbsp.	flour
1 tbsp.	paprika
½ tsp.	salt
¼ tsp.	pepper
1 lb.	boneless lean pork, cut in 1-inch cubes
4 tsp.	olive oil
2 cans	(14½ oz. *each*) DEL MONTE® Original Recipe Stewed Tomatoes
½ cup	sour cream, room temperature

■ Combine flour, paprika, salt and pepper. Toss with meat.

■ In skillet, brown meat in oil over medium-high heat. Stir in tomatoes. Cook, uncovered, over medium heat 20 minutes or until meat is tender, stirring frequently. Remove pan from heat.

■ Remove ½ cup of sauce mixture from skillet and blend with sour cream. Return mixture to skillet; blend well. *Do not boil.*

■ Serve over hot cooked noodles and garnish with chopped parsley, if desired.

4 servings

Greek Lamb Shanks

¼ cup	oil
6	medium lamb shanks (4 to 5 lb.), trim fat
1 can	(14 oz.) chicken broth
1 can	(6 oz.) DEL MONTE Tomato Paste
⅓ cup	molasses
⅓ cup	lemon juice
2 tsp.	salt
½ tsp.	pepper
½ tsp.	rosemary, crumbled
½ tsp.	oregano
2	cloves garlic, crushed
6	carrots, cut into 1-inch chunks

■ In Dutch oven, heat oil and brown lamb shanks on all sides; drain excess fat.

■ In bowl, mix chicken broth, tomato paste, molasses, lemon juice, salt, pepper, rosemary, oregano and garlic. Pour mixture over shanks. Add carrots.

■ Cover tightly and simmer 2 to 2½ hours or until meat is fork-tender. Stir occasionally, adding more chicken broth, if necessary, to prevent sticking.

■ With slotted spoon, remove shanks and carrots to platter.

■ Skim fat from broth. Pour juice over shanks. Serve with noodles, if desired.

6 servings

Hungarian Pork Paprika

Tabbouli Lamb Sandwich

1 can	(14½ oz.) DEL MONTE® Original Recipe Stewed Tomatoes
½ cup	bulgur wheat
1½ cups	cooked, diced lamb *or* beef
¾ cup	diced cucumber
3 tbsp.	minced fresh mint *or* parsley
1 tbsp.	fresh lemon juice
1 tbsp.	olive oil
3	pita breads, cut in halves

■ Drain tomatoes reserving liquid; pour liquid into measuring cup. Add water, if needed, to measure ¾ cup.

■ In small saucepan, bring liquid to boil. Stir in bulgur; cover and simmer 20 minutes or until done. Cool.

■ Chop tomatoes. In medium bowl, combine tomatoes with meat, cucumber, mint, lemon juice and oil. Stir in cooled bulgur. Season with salt and pepper, if desired.

■ Spoon about ½ cup tabbouli into each half pocket bread.

6 half pocket sandwiches

1. *Sitr bulgur into boiling liquid. Cover and simmer for 20 minutes.*

2. *Chop drained tomatoes into small pieces.*

3. *Carefully spoon tabbouli into pita pockets.*

Dijon Lamb Stew

½ lb.	boneless lamb, cut into small pieces
½	onion, chopped
½ tsp.	rosemary
1 tbsp.	olive oil
1 can	(14½ oz.) DEL MONTE® Italian Recipe Stewed Tomatoes
1	carrot, julienne cut
1 tbsp.	Dijon mustard
1 can	(15 oz.) white beans *or* pinto beans, drained

■ In skillet, brown meat, onion and rosemary in oil over medium-high heat, stirring occasionally. Season with salt and pepper, if desired.

■ Add tomatoes, carrot and mustard.

■ Cover and cook over medium heat, 10 minutes; add beans. Cook, uncovered, over medium heat 5 minutes, stirring occasionally.

■ Garnish with sliced ripe olives and chopped parsley, if desired.

4 servings

Bayou Dirty Rice

¼ lb.	hot sausage, crumbled
½	onion, chopped
1	stalk celery, sliced
1 pkg.	(6 oz.) wild and long grain rice seasoned mix
1 can	(14½ oz.) DEL MONTE® Cajun Recipe Stewed Tomatoes
½	green bell pepper chopped
¼ cup	chopped parsley

■ In skillet, brown sausage and onion over medium-high heat; drain. Add celery, rice and rice seasoning packet; cook and stir 2 minutes.

■ Drain tomatoes reserving liquid; pour into measuring cup. Add water to liquid to measure 1⅓ cups; pour over rice. Add tomatoes; bring to boil. Cover and cook over low heat 20 minutes.

■ Add pepper and parsley. Cover and cook 5 minutes or until rice is tender.

■ Serve with roasted chicken or Cornish game hens, if desired.

4 to 6 servings

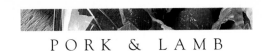
Pork Sauté

¾ lb.	boneless pork loin
1 can	(15 oz.) DEL MONTE® Lite Sliced Bartlett Pears
2 tbsp.	white wine vinegar
½ tsp.	ground ginger
1 tsp.	red pepper flakes
1 tsp.	coriander
1 cup	chopped onion
1	clove garlic, minced
1 tbsp.	oil
1 can	(14½ oz.) DEL MONTE Cut Green Beans, drained
½ cup	thin diagonal sliced carrots
2 tsp.	cornstarch
½ cup	chicken broth

■ Partially freeze meat and slice paper thin across the grain. Drain fruit reserving liquid. To reserved liquid, add vinegar, ginger, pepper and coriander. Add meat; marinate 1 hour or more.

■ In skillet, cook onion and garlic in hot oil until softened. Thoroughly drain meat, reserving marinade.

■ Add meat to skillet and sauté, stirring constantly until browned. Reduce heat; stir in green beans and carrots.

■ Dissolve cornstarch in chicken broth and remaining marinade. Add to skillet; cook, stirring constantly, until thickened and translucent. Add fruit and toss lightly.

4 to 6 servings

Ham in Peach Sauce

1 can	(5 lb.) cooked ham Whole cloves
2 cans	(15¼ oz. *each*) DEL MONTE Sliced Yellow Cling Peaches, drained
1 jar	(10 oz.) apricot preserves
1 cup	dry sherry
1 tsp.	grated orange peel
¼ tsp.	allspice

■ Place ham in 13 x 9 x 2-inch baking dish. Score ham and insert cloves. In blender container, combine remaining ingredients; cover and blend until smooth. Pour over ham.

■ Bake at 325°F, one hour, basting occasionally. Remove ham to serving platter; serve with sauce.

■ Garnish with lemon slices and parsley, if desired. Can be served hot or cold.

10 servings

Peachy Jamaican Pork

1 lb.	pork tenderloin *or* loin, trimmed and sliced ¼-inch thick
1 tbsp.	vegetable oil
3 tbsp.	nonfat dry milk
2 tsp.	coffee crystals
	Dash pepper
1 can	(15 oz.) DEL MONTE® Lite Sliced Peaches *or* Apricot Halves
2 tbsp.	chopped parsley

■ In large skillet, brown meat in oil; remove and keep warm. Combine milk, coffee crystals and pepper with 3 tablespoons water.

■ Drain fruit reserving liquid in skillet. Add coffee mixture. Cook over high heat 3 minutes to reduce and thicken liquid.

■ Return meat to skillet; simmer 4 to 6 minutes, turning frequently. Add fruit and parsley. Cover and heat through.

4 servings

Sweet and Sour Pork Chops

1 can	(8 oz.) DEL MONTE Sliced Pineapple In Its Own Juice
4	pork chops, ½-inch thick
1 tbsp.	oil
¼ cup	DEL MONTE Tomato Ketchup
3 tbsp.	firmly packed brown sugar
1 tsp.	cornstarch
½ tsp.	salt
¼ tsp.	pepper

■ Drain pineapple reserving juice. Brown meat in hot oil; drain. Top with pineapple.

■ Combine reserved juice, ketchup, sugar, cornstarch, salt and pepper; pour over meat. Cover and simmer 20 minutes.

■ Garnish with sliced green onions, if desired.

4 servings

Festive Pork Salad

1 can	(14½ oz.) DEL MONTE® Mexican Recipe Stewed Tomatoes, cut up
1 pkg.	(1¼ oz.) taco seasoning mix
4	cooked pork chops, cut into thin strips
1 can	(8¾ oz.) DEL MONTE Whole Kernel Golden Sweet Corn, drained
1	large head romaine lettuce
1 cup	(4 oz.) shredded Cheddar cheese
	Tortilla chips, coarsely broken

■ In large skillet, cook tomatoes and taco seasoning until thickened, about 5 minutes. Add meat and corn; toss to coat.

■ Place lettuce in salad bowl; top with meat mixture.

■ Sprinkle with cheese and tortilla chips. Garnish with sour cream and sliced green onions, if desired. Serve with hot buttered flour tortillas.

4 to 6 servings

*H*alibut Bake

4	halibut steaks
1 can	(8 oz.) DEL MONTE® Tomato Sauce
¼ cup	sliced ripe olives
1 tbsp.	minced onion
1 tsp.	basil
¼ tsp.	sugar
	Dash garlic powder
	Pepper

■ Season fish with pepper and lemon juice, if desired; place in shallow 2-quart baking dish. Combine remaining ingredients; pour over fish.

■ Bake at 350°F, 35 to 40 minutes or until fish flakes easily with fork. Serve with lemon wedges, if desired.

4 servings

Spa Fish Cakes with Marinara Salsa

1 can	(14½ oz.) DEL MONTE® Italian Recipe Stewed Tomatoes
½ cup	sliced green onions
⅛ tsp.	garlic powder
3½ cups	cooked, flaked fish (halibut, salmon *or* snapper)
2	eggs, beaten
½ cup	Italian seasoned dry bread crumbs
4 tsp.	light mayonnaise
⅛ tsp.	cayenne pepper
1 tbsp.	butter

■ Drain tomatoes reserving ¼ cup liquid. Chop tomatoes; combine with ¼ cup onions and garlic powder.

■ In bowl, combine fish, eggs, crumbs, mayonnaise, cayenne pepper remaining ¼ cup onions and ⅓ cup tomato mixture. Form into 8 patties.

■ Cook in butter over medium-low heat until golden brown. Add reserved liquid to remaining tomato mixture; spoon over patties.

■ Serve with hot pepper sauce, if desired.

4 servings (2 patties each)

Grilled Fish with Gazpacho Salsa

1 can	(14½ oz.) DEL MONTE® Original Recipe Stewed Tomatoes
¼ cup	DEL MONTE Picante or Traditional Salsa, Hot
¼ cup	fresh lime *or* lemon juice
1¼ lb.	red snapper, halibut *or* salmon
⅓ cup	diced cucumber
⅓ cup	sliced green onions
¼ cup	diced green bell pepper
1 tsp.	oil

■ Drain tomatoes reserving juice. Combine reserved juice, salsa and lime juice. Pour half over fish; marinate ½ hour. Coarsely chop tomatoes; combine with remaining marinade, cucumber, onions, green bell pepper and oil. Chill.

■ Remove fish; season to taste with salt and pepper, if desired.

■ Cook over hot coals 2 to 3 minutes per side or until fish flakes easily with a fork.

■ Top fish with salsa. Garnish with chopped cilantro and lime wedges, if desired.

4 servings

HELPFUL HINT:
In warm weather, refrigerate fish while marinating.

*H*alibut Tomato Stew

1	clove garlic, minced
½ tsp.	tarragon, crushed
1 tbsp.	olive oil
1 can	(14½ oz.) DEL MONTE® Stewed Tomatoes (No Salt Added)
½ cup	dry white wine
1 lb.	halibut, cut in ¾-inch cubes
½ cup	green bell pepper strips
1 can	(15¼ oz.) DEL MONTE Sweet Peas (No Salt Added), drained

■ In skillet, cook garlic and tarragon in oil 1 minute. Add tomatoes and wine; bring to boil. Simmer, uncovered 10 minutes or until liquid is almost gone.

■ Add fish and peppers. Cover and cook 5 minutes.

■ Gently stir in peas; heat through. *Do not boil.*

■ Serve over rice and garnish with sliced green onions, if desired.

5 servings

HELPFUL HINT:
Before cooking, thoroughly rinse fish under cold water.

Quick Mediterranean Fish *(Microwave)*

1	medium onion, sliced
2 tbsp.	olive oil
1	clove garlic, crushed
1 can	(14 oz.) DEL MONTE® Italian Recipe Stewed Tomatoes
¼ cup	DEL MONTE Thick & Chunky Salsa, Medium
¼ tsp.	ground cinnamon
1½ lb.	firm fish (halibut, red snapper *or* seabass)
12	stuffed green olives, halved crosswise

■ In 1½ quart microwavable dish, combine onion, oil and garlic. Cover and cook on HIGH 3 minutes; drain.

■ Stir in tomatoes, salsa and cinnamon. Top with fish and olives. Cover and cook on HIGH 3 to 4 minutes or until fish flakes easily with fork.

4 to 6 servings

New England Fisherman's Skillet

4	small red potatoes, diced
1	onion, chopped
1 tbsp.	olive oil
2	stalks celery, chopped
2	cloves garlic, minced
½ tsp.	thyme, crushed
1 can	(14½ oz.) DEL MONTE® Stewed Tomatoes (No Salt Added)
1 lb.	firm white fish (such as halibut, snapper *or* cod)

■ In skillet, brown potatoes and onion in oil over medium-high heat, stirring occasionally. Season with salt-free herb seasoning mix, if desired.

■ Stir in celery, garlic, and thyme; cook 4 minutes. Add tomatoes; bring to boil. Cook 4 minutes or until thickened.

■ Add fish; cover and cook over medium heat 5 to 8 minutes or until fish flakes easily with fork.

■ Garnish with lemon wedges and chopped parsley, if desired.

4 servings

1. Brown potatoes and onions in oil over medium-high heat.

2. Add tomatoes to garlic, celery and thyme. Cook until thickened.

3. Add fish, cover and cook until fish flakes easily.

Fish Françoise

1 can	(14½ oz.) DEL MONTE® Original Recipe Stewed Tomatoes
1 tbsp.	lemon juice
2	cloves garlic, minced
½ tsp.	tarragon, crushed
⅛ tsp.	pepper
3 tbsp.	whipping cream
	Oil
1½ lb.	firm white fish (such as halibut *or* cod)
	Lemon wedges

■ Preheat broiler; position rack 4 inches from heat. In saucepan, combine tomatoes, lemon juice, garlic, tarragon and pepper. Cook, uncovered, over medium-high heat about 10 minutes or until liquid is evaporated.

■ Add cream. Cook over low heat 5 minutes until very thick; set aside.

■ Brush broiler pan with oil. Arrange fish on pan; season with salt and pepper, if desired. Broil fish 3 to 4 minutes per side or until fish flakes easily with fork.

■ Spread tomato mixture over top of fish. Broil 1 minute. Serve immediately with lemon wedges.

4 servings

Grilled Prawns with Salsa Vera Cruz

Grilled Prawns with Salsa Vera Cruz

1 can	(14½ oz.) DEL MONTE® Mexican Recipe Stewed Tomatoes
1	orange, peeled and chopped
¼ cup	sliced green onions
¼ cup	chopped cilantro *or* parsley
1 tbsp.	olive oil
1 tsp.	minced jalapeño chile
1	small clove garlic, crushed
1 lb.	medium shrimp, peeled and deveined

■ Drain tomatoes reserving liquid. Chop tomatoes.

■ In medium bowl, combine tomatoes with reserved liquid, orange, onion, cilantro, oil, jalapeño and garlic. Season to taste with salt and pepper, if desired.

■ Thread shrimp on skewers; season with salt and pepper, if desired.

■ Brush grill with oil. Cook over hot coals about 3 minutes per side or until shrimp turn opaque pink. Serve with salsa.

4 servings

HELPFUL HINT:
Thoroughly rinse shrimp in cold water before cooking.

Milano Shrimp Fettucine

4 oz.	spinach *or* egg fettuccine
½ lb.	medium shrimp, peeled and deveined
1	clove garlic, minced
1 tbsp.	olive oil
1 can	(14½ oz.) DEL MONTE Pasta Style Chunky Tomatoes
½ cup	whipping cream
¼ cup	sliced green onions

■ Cook fettuccine according to package directions; drain.

■ Sauté shrimp with garlic in oil until shrimp are pink.

■ Stir in tomatoes; simmer 5 minutes. Blend in cream and green onions; heat through. *Do not boil.* Serve over cooked pasta.

3 to 4 servings

Napolitano Skillet Pasta

½ lb.	Italian sausage, sliced or crumbled
1	large onion, coarsely chopped
1	large clove garlic, minced
½ tsp.	fennel seed
2 cans	(14½ oz. *each*) DEL MONTE® Italian Recipe Stewed Tomatoes
1 can	(8 oz.) DEL MONTE Tomato Sauce
1 cup	water
8 oz.	uncooked rigatoni *or* spiral pasta
8	mushrooms, sliced
	Grated Parmesan cheese
	Chopped parsley

■ Brown sausage in large skillet. Add onion, garlic and fennel seed. Cook until onion is soft; drain.

■ Stir in stewed tomatoes, tomato sauce, water and pasta. Cover and bring to a boil; reduce heat to low. Simmer, covered, 25 to 30 minutes or until pasta is tender, stirring occasionally.

■ Stir in mushrooms; simmer 5 minutes. Serve in skillet garnished with cheese and parsley.

4 servings

Fettuccine with Tomatoes and Zucchini

6 oz.	fettuccine
½ lb.	ground beef
½	onion, chopped
1 tsp.	tarragon, crushed
1 can	(14½ oz.) DEL MONTE® Original Recipe Stewed Tomatoes
1 can	(8 oz.) DEL MONTE Tomato Sauce
1	medium carrot, julienne cut
1	medium zucchini, cubed

■ Cook pasta according to package directions; drain. In skillet, brown meat with onion and tarragon. Add tomatoes, tomato sauce and carrots.

■ Cook, uncovered, over medium heat 8 minutes, stirring occasionally. Add zucchini; cover and cook 7 minutes or until zucchini is tender.

■ Just before serving, spoon sauce over hot pasta. Garnish with chopped parsley, if desired.

4 to 6 servings

HELPFUL HINT:
Pasta may be cooked ahead and rinsed in cold water. It may then be frozen or refrigerated and reheated in boiling water or in the microwave oven.

*P*asta Pronto

8 oz.	linguine *or* spaghetti, uncooked
1 lb.	ground beef, ground turkey *or* mild Italian sausage
1 cup	coarsely chopped onions
1	clove garlic, minced
2 cans	(14½ oz. *each*) DEL MONTE® Pasta Style Chunky Tomatoes, undrained
1 can	(8 oz.) DEL MONTE Tomato Sauce
¼ cup	(1 oz.) grated Parmesan cheese

■ Cook pasta according to package directions; drain and keep hot.

■ In large skillet brown meat with onions and garlic; drain.

■ Add tomatoes and tomato sauce. Cook, stirring frequently, 15 minutes.

■ Spoon sauce over hot pasta; sprinkle with cheese. Serve with bread and a tossed salad, if desired.

4 servings

Country Style Lasagna

9	2-inch wide lasagna noodles
2 cans	(14½ oz. *each*) DEL MONTE® Pasta Style Chunky Tomatoes
	Milk
2 tbsp.	butter *or* margarine
3 tbsp.	flour
1 tsp.	basil, crushed
1 cup	diced cooked ham
2 cups	shredded mozzarella cheese

■ Cook pasta according to package directions; rinse and drain.

■ Drain tomatoes reserving liquid; pour liquid into measuring cup. Add milk to measure 2 cups.

■ In saucepan, melt butter; stir in flour and basil. Cook, stirring constantly, over medium heat 3 minutes. Stir in reserved liquid; cook, stirring constantly, until thickened. Season with salt and pepper, if desired. Stir in tomatoes.

■ Spread thin layer of sauce on bottom of 7 x 12-inch or 2-quart baking dish. Top with ⅓ each of noodles, sauce, ham, then cheese; repeat twice.

■ Bake uncovered at 375°F, 25 minutes. Garnish with grated Parmesan cheese or sliced green onions, if desired.

6 servings

Eggplant Pasta Bake

2 cups	(4 oz.) bow-tie pasta
1 lb.	eggplant, diced
1	clove garlic, minced
¼ cup	olive oil
1½ cups	shredded Monterey Jack cheese
1 cup	sliced green onions
½ cup	grated Parmesan cheese
1 can	(14½ oz.) DEL MONTE® Pasta Style Chunky Tomatoes

■ Cook pasta according to package directions; drain.

■ In skillet, sauté eggplant and garlic in oil until tender. Toss eggplant with cooked pasta, 1 cup Monterey Jack cheese, green onions and Parmesan cheese.

■ Place in greased 9-inch square baking dish. Top with tomatoes and remaining ½ cup Monterey Jack cheese.

■ Bake at 350°F, 15 minutes or until heated through.

6 servings

1. Sauté eggplant and garlic in oil until tender.

2. Mix cooked pasta, green onions and cheeses with eggplant.

3. Place mixture in baking dish and top with tomatoes and remaining cheese.

Skillet Beans and Noodle Toss

1	clove garlic, minced
½ tsp.	salt-free herb and spice seasoning
¼ tsp.	rosemary, crushed
2 tsp.	olive oil
1 can	(14½ oz.) DEL MONTE® Cut Green Beans (No Salt Added)
1 can	(14½ oz.) DEL MONTE Stewed Tomatoes (No Salt Added)
½ cup	uncooked penne *or* other tube pasta

■ In skillet, cook garlic with herb and spice seasoning and rosemary in oil, 1 minute.

■ Drain beans reserving liquid in skillet. Add tomatoes; bring to boil. Cook, uncovered over medium heat, 10 minutes.

■ Stir in noodles. Reduce heat; cover and cook about 18 minutes, adding beans during last 5 minutes.

4 to 6 servings

*R*avioli *Bake Parmesano*

1 pkg.	**(12 oz.) fresh or frozen cheese ravioli**
½ lb.	**lean ground beef**
½	**onion, finely chopped**
2	**cloves garlic, minced**
½ tsp.	**oregano, crushed**
1 can	**(14½ oz.) DEL MONTE® Italian Recipe Stewed Tomatoes**
1 can	**(14½ oz.) DEL MONTE Zucchini With Italian-Style Tomato Sauce**
½ cup	**shredded Parmesan cheese**

■ Cook pasta according to package directions; rinse and drain. In skillet, brown meat with onion, garlic and oregano; drain.

■ Add tomatoes. Cook, uncovered, over medium-high heat 15 minutes or until thickened, stirring occasionally. Add zucchini; heat through.

■ In oiled 2-quart microwavable dish, arrange ½ pasta; top with ½ sauce and ½ cheese. Repeat.

■ Cover and cook on HIGH in microwave 8 minutes or until heated through, rotating once.

4 servings

Garden Primavera Pasta

6 oz.	bow-tie pasta
1 jar	(6 oz.) marinated artichoke hearts
2	cloves garlic, minced
½ tsp.	rosemary, crushed
1	green pepper, cut in thin strips
1	large carrot, cut in 2-inch julienne strips
1	medium zucchini, cut in 2-inch julienne strips
1 can	(14½ oz.) DEL MONTE® Pasta Style Chunky Tomatoes
12	small ripe pitted olives (optional)

■ Cook pasta according to package directions; drain.

■ Toss pasta in 3 tablespoons artichoke marinade; set aside. Cut artichoke hearts in halves.

■ In large skillet, cook garlic and rosemary in 1 tablespoon artichoke marinade. Add remaining ingredients, except pasta, artichokes and olives.

■ Cook, uncovered, over medium-high heat 4 to 5 minutes or until vegetables are tender-crisp and sauce is thickened. Add artichokes and olives.

■ Spoon over pasta. Serve with grated Parmesan cheese, if desired.

4 servings

Mediterranean Pasta

6 to 8 oz.	vermicelli pasta
2	half boneless chicken breasts, skinned, cut in ½ x 1½-inch strips
4	slices bacon, diced
1 can	(14½ oz.) DEL MONTE® Pasta Style Chunky Tomatoes
1 can	(15 oz.) DEL MONTE Tomato Sauce
½ tsp.	rosemary, crushed
1 pkg.	(9 oz.) frozen artichoke hearts, thawed
½ cup	ripe pitted olives, sliced lengthwise

■ Cook pasta according to package directions; drain. Season chicken with salt and pepper, if desired.

■ In skillet, cook bacon until almost crisp; add chicken. Brown chicken on both sides over medium-high heat; drain.

■ Stir in tomatoes, tomato sauce and rosemary. Cook, uncovered, 15 minutes, stirring occasionally. Add artichokes and olives; heat through.

■ Just before serving, spoon sauce over hot pasta. Garnish with crumbled feta cheese and chopped parsley, if desired.

4 to 6 servings

HELPFUL HINT:
To cook pasta ahead, cook, rinse well and drain. Cover and refrigerate. Just before serving, dip in boiling water to reheat or sprinkle with water and heat in microwave.

Creamy Asparagus Pasta

1 can	(15 oz.) DEL MONTE® Tender Green Asparagus Spears
2 tbsp.	butter *or* margarine
2 tbsp.	flour
½ tsp.	basil
1 cup	heavy cream *or* half-and-half *or* milk
½ cup	Parmesan cheese
⅛ tsp.	white pepper
8 oz.	fettuccine, cooked

■ Drain asparagus reserving liquid; set aside. Purée asparagus in food processor or blender.

■ In medium saucepan, melt butter. Blend in flour and basil; cook 1 minute. Add cream; bring to boil. Cook, stirring constantly, until thickened.

■ Add asparagus, cheese, pepper and ½ cup reserved liquid. Heat through. Toss with hot cooked pasta.

4 to 6 servings (2½ cups sauce)

Pasta with Ham and Tomatoes

6 oz.	mostaccioli pasta
1 cup	julienne cooked ham
½ tsp.	rosemary, crushed
1 can	(14½ oz.) DEL MONTE Pasta Style Chunky Tomatoes
1 can	(8 oz.) DEL MONTE Tomato Sauce
1	clove garlic, minced
½ cup	sliced green onions
⅓ cup	heavy cream

■ Cook pasta according to package directions; drain. In skillet, lightly brown ham with rosemary, stirring frequently.

■ Stir in tomatoes, tomato sauce and garlic. Simmer, uncovered, 15 minutes.

■ Stir in onions and cream. Heat through; *do not boil.*

■ Just before serving, spoon sauce over hot pasta. Garnish with additional green onions and grated Parmesan cheese, if desired.

4 servings

HELPFUL HINT:
Refrigerate leftovers promptly; if possible, store sauce and noodles separately.

Rosemary Turkey Pizza

1 can	(14½ oz.) DEL MONTE® Italian Recipe Stewed Tomatoes
1½ cups	bite-size cooked turkey
½ tsp.	rosemary, crushed
1	(12-inch) prepared, pre-baked pizza crust
2 cups	(8 oz.) shredded mozzarella cheese, divided
1	green, yellow *or* red bell pepper, sliced
⅓ cup	sliced green onions

■ Preheat oven to 450°F. Drain tomatoes, reserving liquid. In medium skillet, combine reserved liquid with turkey and rosemary. Cook 5 minutes or until liquid is evaporated.

■ Place crust on baking sheet. Chop tomatoes; spread evenly over crust. Cover with half of cheese; top with turkey mixture, pepper slices and green onions. Sprinkle with remaining 1 cup cheese.

■ Bake 10 minutes or until cheese is hot and bubbly.

4 to 6 servings

HELPFUL HINT:
Refrigerated pizza dough is every bit as good as your favorite pizzeria's. For best results, be sure to follow the package directions.

Fiesta Pizza (top), Pizza Turnovers

Fiesta Pizza

½ lb.	chorizo sausage, sliced, *or* ground beef
1 can	(14½ oz.) DEL MONTE® Mexican Recipe Stewed Tomatoes
½ tsp.	ground cumin
8 oz.	(2 cups) shredded Monterey Jack cheese
1	small onion, thinly sliced
1	small green bell pepper, thinly sliced
1 can	(4 oz.) diced green chiles
1	(12-inch) prepared, pre-baked pizza crust

■ Preheat oven to 425°F. In skillet, cook sausage; drain. Thoroughly drain tomatoes reserving liquid; add reserved liquid and cumin to skillet.

■ Cook, stirring constantly, until thickened. Coarsely chop tomatoes.

■ Place crust on baking sheet. Top with ½ cheese, sausage mixture, tomatoes, onion, pepper, chiles and remaining cheese.

■ Bake 12 to 15 minutes or until hot and bubbly.

4 to 6 servings

Variation:
For spicier pizza, use jalapeño Jack cheese.

Pizza Turnovers

1 can	(14½ oz.) DEL MONTE Italian Recipe Stewed Tomatoes
4 tsp.	cornstarch
1 can	(4 oz.) sliced mushrooms, drained
1 pkg.	(10 oz.) refrigerated pizza dough
1 cup	(4 oz.) shredded mozzarella cheese
1 pkg.	(6 oz.) thinly sliced fully cooked ham

■ In medium saucepan, combine tomatoes and cornstarch. Cook over medium heat stirring constantly until thickened and translucent. Stir in mushrooms.

■ Unroll pizza dough on cutting board. Press into 12-inch square. Cut into four 6 x 6-inch squares.

■ For each square, sprinkle ¼ cup mozzarella cheese onto diagonal half; top with ¼ of ham slices and spoon ¼ cup tomato mixture over ham.

■ Diagonally fold dough over to form triangle, using fork to seal edges. Place turnovers on greased baking sheet. Brush with water and sprinkle with grated Parmesan cheese, if desired.

■ Bake at 425°F, 10 to 15 minutes or until golden. Reheat remaining sauce. Serve with turnovers.

4 servings

Pineapple Cole Slaw

⅔ cup	sour cream
⅔ cup	mayonnaise
1 tbsp.	celery seed
4 cups	shredded cabbage
2 cups	miniature marshmallows
2 cups	sliced green grapes
1 can	(15¼ oz.) DEL MONTE® Pineapple Chunks In Its Own Juice, drained

■ Thoroughly mix sour cream, mayonnaise and celery seed; toss lightly with cabbage, marshmallows, grapes and pineapple.

■ Chill several hours; toss lightly before serving.

8 to 10 servings

Deluxe Spinach and Peach Salad

1 can	(15¼ oz.) DEL MONTE Sliced Yellow Cling Peaches
⅓ cup	olive oil
1 tbsp.	white wine vinegar
1 tsp.	prepared mustard
½ tsp.	salt
⅛ tsp.	pepper
	Dash ground cloves
6 cups	loosely packed fresh spinach leaves
1	large avocado, peeled, pitted and sliced
¼ cup	diced cooked bacon
¼ cup	cashews

■ Drain peaches reserving 2 tablespoons syrup. Combine reserved syrup, oil, vinegar, mustard, salt, pepper and cloves; mix well.

■ In large salad bowl, combine spinach, fruit, avocado, bacon and nuts. Just before serving, gently toss with dressing.

4 to 6 servings

Gorgonzola Green Bean Salad

⅓ cup	Gorgonzola *or* blue cheese
3 tbsp.	olive oil
2 tbsp.	red wine vinegar
1 can	(14½ oz.) DEL MONTE® Cut Green Beans, drained
1 cup	cherry tomatoes, halved
½ cup	chopped walnuts
¼ cup	sliced green onions

■ In bowl, mash cheese with oil and vinegar. Toss with beans, tomatoes, nuts and onions.

■ Serve on a bed of Romaine lettuce, if desired. Add salt and pepper to taste.

4 servings

Calypso Rice Salad

1 can	(14½ oz.) DEL MONTE® Stewed Tomatoes (No Salt Added)
1 cup	uncooked long-grain white rice
⅓ cup	nonfat plain yogurt
3 tbsp.	light mayonnaise
2 tbsp.	fresh lemon juice
1 tbsp.	curry powder
½ cup	sliced green onions
¼ cup	DEL MONTE Seedless Raisins

■ Drain tomatoes reserving liquid; pour into measuring cup.

■ Add water to reserved liquid to measure 2 cups; pour into saucepan. Bring to boil. Add rice; reduce heat. Cover and simmer 20 minutes until rice it tender; cool.

■ In large bowl, combine tomatoes, yogurt, mayonnaise, lemon juice and curry powder. Stir in onions, raisins and rice; chill.

■ Garnish with chopped parsley and toasted slivered almonds, if desired.

6 servings

Green Bean and Olive Salad

2 cans	(14½ oz. *each*) DEL MONTE® Cut Green Beans, drained
1 can	(14½ oz.) DEL MONTE Original Recipe Stewed Tomatoes
1 cup	pitted medium ripe olives
1 cup	sliced fresh mushrooms
½ cup	olive *or* vegetable oil
1 tbsp.	vinegar
1 tsp.	prepared mustard
½ tsp.	thyme
¼ tsp.	pepper
2 tbsp.	minced parsley
	lettuce leaves

■ In bowl, gently toss green beans, tomatoes, olives and mushrooms. Combine oil, vinegar, mustard, thyme and pepper; mix until well blended.

■ Pour dressing over vegetables; cover and marinate at least 1 hour. Just before serving, toss with parsley.

■ Serve on lettuce leaves. Garnish with lemon slices, if desired. (Can be made a day ahead.)

8 to 10 servings

Beet and Pear Salad

1 can	(15¼ oz.) DEL MONTE® Bartlett Pear Halves
1 can	(14½ oz.) DEL MONTE Sliced Beets, drained
½ cup	thinly sliced red onion
2 tbsp.	vegetable oil
1 tbsp.	white wine vinegar
⅓ cup	crumbled blue cheese

■ Drain fruit reserving 1 tablespoon syrup.

■ Cut pears in half lengthwise. Place pears, beets and onion in serving dish.

■ Whisk together oil, vinegar and reserved syrup. Pour over salad; toss gently.

■ Just before serving, add cheese and toss. Serve on bed of Romaine lettuce leaves, if desired.

4 to 6 servings

Sweet and Sour Asparagus Salad

1 can	**(15 oz.) DEL MONTE® Tender Green Asparagus Spears, drained**
3	**slices bacon, diced**
⅓ cup	**julienne red *or* green bell pepper**
¼ cup	**chopped onion**
2 tbsp.	**white wine vinegar**
2 tsp.	**sugar**

■ Arrange asparagus on serving dish.

■ Cook bacon until crisp. Stir in pepper and onion. Cook 1 minute. Spoon bacon mixture over asparagus with 1 tablespoon bacon drippings.

■ Combine vinegar and sugar. Drizzle over vegetables. Serve immediately.

4 servings

Microwave Directions: Arrange asparagus on serving dish. In 1-quart microwavable dish, cover bacon with paper towel. Cook on HIGH 3 minutes or until crisp, stirring halfway through. Stir in pepper and onion. Cover and cook 30 seconds.

Spoon bacon mixture over asparagus with 1 tablespoon bacon drippings. Combine vinegar and sugar. Drizzle over vegetables. Serve immediately.

Taco Corn Salad

1 lb.	lean ground beef
½ cup	chopped green onion
2½ tsp.	chili powder
1½ tsp.	oregano, crushed
½ tsp.	salt
1 can	(15¼ oz.) DEL MONTE® Whole Kernel Golden Sweet Corn, drained
1	medium head iceberg lettuce, shredded
1	tomato, cut into wedges
	Tortilla chips
	Sliced avocado *or* guacamole
	Taco Salsa Dressing (see recipe below)

■ Cook meat and onion in skillet until meat is browned; drain. Stir in chili powder, oregano and salt. Reduce heat; simmer 5 to 10 minutes. Add corn. Cover and chill. Line salad bowl with lettuce.

■ Top with meat mixture. Garnish with tomato, tortilla chips and avocado. Serve with Taco Salsa Dressing.

4 to 6 servings

Microwave Directions: Crumble meat into 2-quart glass baking dish. Add onion. Cook on HIGH, covered for 3 minutes, stirring once halfway through. Drain. Stir in corn, chili powder, oregano and salt. Cook, covered, 3 minutes. Chill. Line salad bowl with lettuce. Top with meat mixture. Garnish with tomato, corn chips and avocado. Serve with Taco Salsa Dressing.

Variation:
Substitude 1 package (1½ oz.) taco season mix for chili powder, oregano and salt.

Taco Salsa Dressing

½ cup	DEL MONTE Thick & Chunky Salsa, Mild *or* Medium
3 tbsp.	red wine vinegar
¼ cup	oil
1 tbsp.	minced cilantro (optional)
¼ tsp.	oregano

■ Combine ingredients; mix well.

Makes approximately 1 cup

Creamed Beans and Potatoes

1 can	(14½ oz.) DEL MONTE® Cut Green Beans
1 can	(14½ oz.) DEL MONTE Whole New Potatoes
1 can	(3 oz.) sliced mushrooms
2 tbsp.	butter *or* margarine
2 tbsp.	flour
1 cup	milk
¼ tsp.	basil
¼ tsp.	rosemary
¼ tsp.	salt
	Dash pepper

■ Drain beans, potatoes and mushrooms; cut potatoes into chunks.

■ Melt butter in saucepan; blend in flour. Blend in milk, basil, rosemary, salt and pepper. Cook, stirring constantly, until thickened.

■ Add vegetables; heat through.

6 servings

Spinach and Potato Italiano

½	medium onion, sliced
4	large mushrooms, quartered
1	clove garlic, minced
1 tsp.	olive oil *or* sweet butter
1	medium carrot, coarsely shredded
1 can	(13½ oz.) DEL MONTE® Whole Leaf Spinach, well drained
1 can	(14½ oz.) DEL MONTE Sliced New Potatoes, drained
2 tbsp.	white wine vinegar

■ In skillet, cook onion, mushrooms and garlic in olive oil until soft. Stir in carrot. Cook until tender-crisp.

■ Stir in spinach, potatoes and vinegar; heat through.

4 servings

Corn and Zucchini Primavera (left), Corn and Carrot Sauté

Corn and Carrot Sauté

1 can	(15¼ oz.) DEL MONTE® Whole Kernel Golden Sweet Corn, drained
1 can	(14½ oz.) DEL MONTE Sliced Carrots, drained
2 tbsp.	butter *or* margarine
	Salt and pepper to taste
2 tbsp.	chopped parsley

■ Sauté vegetables in butter until heated through. Season with salt and pepper. Sprinkle with parsley.

6 to 8 servings

Variation:
Substitute 1 can (14½ oz.) DEL MONTE Whole Kernel White Sweet Corn for Golden Corn.

Corn and Zucchini Primavera

1	small zucchini, sliced
½	onion, chopped
¼ tsp.	dill weed
1 tbsp.	butter or margarine
1 can	(15¼ oz.) DEL MONTE® Whole Kernel Golden Sweet Corn, drained
1 tbsp.	lemon juice

■ Sauté zucchini, onion, and dill weed in butter until onion is soft. Stir in corn and lemon juice; heat through.

4 to 6 servings

Microwave Directions: Place onion and butter in microwavable dish. Cover and cook on HIGH 2 minutes. Stir in remaining ingredients. Cover and cook on HIGH 4 minutes or until hot.

Savory Vegetable Succotash

1 can	(14½ oz.) DEL MONTE Cut Golden Wax Beans
1 can	(14½ oz.) DEL MONTE Original Recipe Stewed Tomatoes
1 can	(11 oz.) DEL MONTE Summer Crisp Vacuum Packed Golden Sweet Corn
2 tbsp.	butter *or* margarine Salt Pepper

■ Combine ingredients in saucepan; heat through. Season with salt and pepper. Thicken with 1½ tablespoons cornstarch*, if desired.

8 servings

*TIP:
If using cornstarch, dissolve in liquid before heating.

Orange Dilly Peas

½ cup	chopped onion
1	clove garlic, minced
2 tbsp.	butter *or* margarine
1 can	(15¼ oz.) DEL MONTE® Sweet Peas
1 tbsp.	cornstarch
¼ cup	orange juice
¼ tsp.	dill weed
½ tsp.	grated orange peel

■ In saucepan, cook onion and garlic in butter until soft.

■ Drain peas reserving ¼ cup liquid. Dissolve cornstarch in reserved liquid; add orange juice and dill weed.

■ Add to onion mixture; cook, stirring constantly, until thickened and translucent.

■ Add peas and orange peel; heat through.

■ Garnish with additional grated orange peel, if desired.

4 servings

Variation:
Substitute 1 can (14½ oz.) DEL MONTE Peas and Carrots for Sweet Peas.

Sweet and Sour Carrots

2 tbsp.	cider vinegar
2 tbsp.	brown sugar
2 tbsp.	DEL MONTE® Tomato Ketchup
⅛ tsp.	ground ginger
⅓ cup	green bell pepper strips
1 can	(14½ oz.) DEL MONTE Sliced Carrots, drained

■ In saucepan, combine vinegar, sugar, ketchup and ginger. Add green pepper; cook until tender.

■ Gently stir in carrots; heat through.

4 servings

Microwave Directions: In 1-quart microwavable dish, combine vinegar, brown sugar, ketchup and ginger. Add green pepper; cover and cook on HIGH 3 to 4 minutes or until tender. Gently stir in carrots. Cook 1 minute or until heated through.

Variation:
Can also be served cold.

Cheesy Almond Green Beans

1 tbsp.	butter *or* margarine
1	clove garlic, minced
½ cup	coarse fresh bread crumbs
¼ cup	chopped almonds, toasted
¼ cup	grated Parmesan cheese
1 can	(14½ oz.) DEL MONTE® Seasoned Green Beans

■ Melt butter in small skillet. Stir in garlic and bread crumbs; cook stirring occasionally until golden brown. Remove from heat; stir in almonds and cheese.

■ Heat beans; drain. Sprinkle crumb topping over vegetables just before serving.

4 servings

HELPFUL HINT:
Crumb mixture may be made ahead and stored in airtight container.

Asparagus Provençale

⅓ cup	green bell pepper strips
¼ cup	sliced onion
1	clove garlic, minced
½ tsp.	basil, crushed
1 tbsp.	olive oil
1 can	(8 oz.) DEL MONTE Original Recipe Stewed Tomatoes
1 can	(15 oz.) DEL MONTE Tender Green Extra Long Asparagus Spears, drained

■ In 10-inch skillet, cook pepper, onion, garlic and basil in oil over medium-high heat until soft. Stir in tomatoes.

■ Cook stirring occasionally, 8 minutes. Season to taste with salt and pepper. Push vegetable mixture to one side.

■ Place asparagus in other side. Cover and heat through. Remove asparagus to serving dish.

■ Spoon sauce over asparagus. Garnish with sliced ripe olives, if desired.

4 servings

*S*avory Green Bean Medley

½ cup	chopped onion
½ cup	red or green pepper strips
2	small zucchini, thinly sliced
1	clove garlic, crushed
1 tbsp.	olive oil
½ tsp.	basil crushed
½ tsp.	oregano, crushed
½ tsp.	salt
⅛ tsp.	pepper
1 can	(16 oz.) DEL MONTE® Blue Lake Whole Green Beans, drained

■ Cook onion, red pepper, zucchini and garlic in oil until tender.

■ Stir in basil, oregano, salt and pepper.

■ Add green beans; heat through.

6 servings

Peach Pear Sabayon

1 can	(15¼ oz.) DEL MONTE® Sliced Yellow Cling Peaches, drained
1 can	(15¼ oz.) DEL MONTE Sliced Bartlett Pears, drained
⅓ cup	dry sherry
3	egg yolks
¾ cup	sifted powdered sugar
	Dash salt
1 cup	whipping cream, whipped

■ In bowl, combine fruit. Sprinkle with 2 tablespoons sherry; toss with fruit. Cover and chill.

■ In top of double boiler, blend egg yolks, sugar and salt until smooth. Blend in remaining sherry. Cook over hot water, stirring constantly, until thickened (about 10 to 12 minutes). Chill.

■ Whip cream until stiff peaks form; fold into egg mixture. Spoon over fruit and serve.

8 servings

HELPFUL HINT:
For proper sauce consistency, sauce should coat back of spoon.

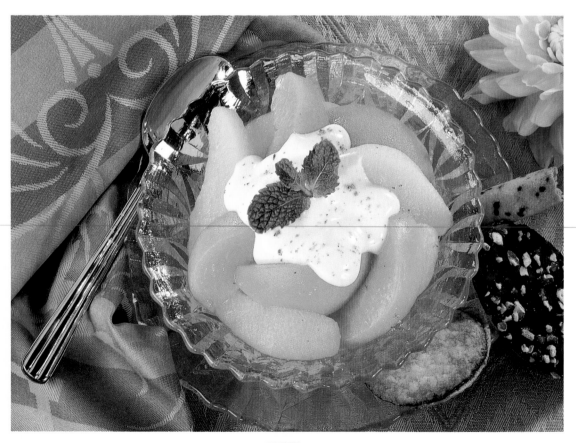

Pears Hélène

1 pt.	**vanilla ice cream**
1 can	**(15¼ oz.) DEL MONTE®** **Bartlett Pear Halves, chilled and drained**
1 can	**(5½ oz.) chocolate syrup, chilled**
	Sliced almonds, toasted (optional)

■ Place 1 scoop of ice cream in each dish. Place pear half, cut side down, on ice cream.

■ Top with chocolate syrup. Garnish with toasted almonds.

6 servings

De-Lite Peach Crème

1 can	**(15 oz.) DEL MONTE Lite Sliced Yellow Cling Peaches**
1 env.	**unflavored gelatin**
1 cup	**plain yogurt**
½ tsp.	**vanilla extract**
1 cup	**frozen non-dairy whipped topping, thawed**

■ Drain peaches and soften gelatin in ½ cup syrup. Dissolve over hot water.

■ Reserve a few peach slices for garnish. Purée the remaining peaches and syrup. Blend in yogurt; add dissolved gelatin and vanilla. Chill until almost set.

■ Fold in whipped topping. Pour into 5-cup mold and chill until firm.

■ Unmold and garnish with peach slices.

6 servings

*B*ourbon St. Ice Cream Topping

1 can	(15¼ oz.) DEL MONTE® Fruit Cocktail *or* 1 can (15¼ oz.) DEL MONTE Sliced Yellow Cling Peaches
1 can	(8 oz.) DEL MONTE Pineapple Chunks In Its Own Juice
⅓ cup	firmly packed brown sugar
4 tsp.	cornstarch
2 tbsp.	butter *or* margarine
2 tsp.	lemon juice
3 tbsp.	rum
½ tsp.	vanilla extract
	Vanilla ice cream

■ Drain fruit reserving liquid in saucepan.

■ Add sugar and cornstarch; stir to dissolve cornstarch. Add butter and lemon juice. Cook, stirring constantly, until thickened.

■ Stir in rum, vanilla and fruits; heat through.

■ Serve warm over ice cream. Garnish with pecans, if desired.

8 servings (approximately 3 cups topping)

Variation:
Substitute 1 can (8¾ oz.) DEL MONTE Sliced Peaches and 1 can (8½ oz.) DEL MONTE Pear Halves for Fruit Cocktail.

*C*reamy Fruit Bavarian

1 pkg.	(3 oz.) cream cheese, softened
¼ cup	sugar
1 can	(15¼ oz.) DEL MONTE Fruit Cocktail, drained
1 can	(8 oz.) DEL MONTE Pineapple Tidbits In Its Own Juice, drained
1 cup	(4 oz.) thawed frozen non-dairy whipped topping
2	DEL MONTE Gel Snack Cups, Strawberry Flavored

■ In medium bowl, blend cream cheese with sugar. Stir in fruit. Gently fold in whipped topping.

■ Cut gel into cubes; gently fold into cream cheese mixture. Cover and chill several hours. Garnish with additional cubes, if desired.

4 to 6 servings

*S*piced Poached Peaches

1 can	(15¼ oz.) DEL MONTE® Yellow Cling Peach Halves
¾ cup	dry red wine
4 tsp.	honey
1	cinnamon stick
2	slices lemon
5 to 6	cloves

■ Drain fruit reserving ¼ cup syrup. Combine reserved syrup, wine, honey, cinnamon and lemon in saucepan. Bring to boil; let simmer 2 minutes.

■ Stud each peach half with a clove and place in wine mixture; simmer 3 minutes. Serve warm.

4 servings

Peaches and Cream

½ cup	whipping cream, whipped
1 cup	peach yogurt
½ tsp.	vanilla extract
¼ tsp.	almond extract
2 cans	(15 oz. *each*) DEL MONTE® Lite Yellow Cling Peach Halves, drained and chilled

■ Combine whipped cream, yogurt and flavorings; chill.

■ In individual dishes, place 2 peach halves and top with yogurt mixture. Garnish with toasted sliced almonds, if desired.

6 to 8 servings

Rum Raisin Peach Melba

1 can	(15¼ oz.) DEL MONTE® Yellow Cling Peach Halves
½ cup	DEL MONTE Seedless Raisins
¼ cup	rum
1 pkg.	(10 oz.) unsweetened frozen raspberries, thawed

■ Drain peaches reserving syrup into saucepan. Bring to boil; cook until syrup is reduced to ⅓ cup. Add raisins and rum. Simmer 1 minute. Remove from heat. Chill.

■ Purée raspberries and push through sieve with spoon to remove seeds.

■ For each serving, spoon 2 to 3 teaspoons raspberry sauce into dessert cup. Place peach half over sauce and spoon rum raisin mixture evenly in center of each peach.

■ Serve with dollop of whipped cream, if desired.

6 servings

Ginger Pear Tart

¾ cup	ginger snap crumbs
¾ cup	vanilla wafer *or* graham cracker crumbs
⅓ cup	butter *or* margarine, melted
1 pkg.	(8 oz.) cream cheese, softened
½ cup	sour cream
¼ cup	sugar
1 can	(15¼ oz.) DEL MONTE Bartlett Pear Halves, drained
2 tbsp.	minced candied ginger
½ tsp.	vanilla extract

■ Combine ginger snap and vanilla wafer crumbs. Stir in butter; mix evenly.

■ Pat into 9-inch tart pan with removable bottom, pushing up sides.

■ Bake at 350°F, 8 minutes; cool. Blend cream cheese, sour cream and sugar until smooth.

■ Reserve 2 pear halves and chop remaining pears. Fold into cream cheese mixture with ginger and vanilla. Spoon into shell: chill until set.

■ Just before serving, garnish with pear fans.

8 servings

HELPFUL HINT:
To make pear fans, cut each pear half in half lengthwise. Make 3 to 4 lengthwise slices in each pear quarter. Fan out on top of tart.

Fruit Cocktail Cream Pie

2 cups	graham cracker crumbs
1/3 cup	butter *or* margarine, melted
1/4 cup	sugar
2 cups	sour cream
2/3 cup	sugar
1 tsp.	grated lemon peel
1 tsp.	lemon juice
1 tsp.	vanilla extract
1 can	(15 1/4 oz.) DEL MONTE® Fruit Cocktail, drained

■ Combine crumbs, butter and 1/4 cup sugar. Reserve 2 tablespoons mixture; press remaining mixture on bottom and sides of 8-inch springform pan.

■ Bake at 350°F, 10 minutes.

■ Combine sour cream, 2/3 cup sugar, lemon peel, lemon juice and vanilla. Reserve 1/4 cup fruit cocktail for garnish. Fold remaining fruit into sour cream mixture. Pour into crust. Top with reserved crumbs.

■ Bake at 350°F, 25 minutes. Cool and chill.

■ Just before serving, garnish with reserved fruit and mint, if desired.

8 to 10 servings

1. *Press crumb mixture on the bottom and up the sides of springform pan.*

2. *Gently fold fruit cocktail into sour cream mixture with spatula.*

3. *Pour into crust. Top with reserved crumbs.*

Lite Peach Pear Tart

Lite Peach Pear Tart

1 can	(15 oz.) DEL MONTE® Lite Sliced Bartlett Pears
1 can	(16 oz.) DEL MONTE Lite Sliced Yellow Cling Peaches
1 env.	unflavored gelatin
1 pkg.	(8 oz.) light cream cheese
1 cup	(8 oz.) vanilla yogurt
1 tsp.	grated lemon peel
1 tsp.	vanilla extract
1	(9-inch) deep dish pie shell, baked

■ Drain fruit reserving 1 cup liquid in small saucepan. Sprinkle gelatin over reserved liquid to soften. Heat, stirring until gelatin is completely dissolved.

■ Blend cream cheese, yogurt, lemon peel and vanilla until smooth. Stir in gelatin mixture. Pour into crust. Cover and chill at least 1 hour or until set.

■ Just before serving, drain fruit on paper towels. Arrange over filling.

■ Garnish with toasted almonds, maraschino cherries and mint leaves, if desired.

6 to 8 servings

Peach Cobbler

2 cans	(15¼ oz. *each*) DEL MONTE Sliced Yellow Cling Peaches
1 cup	sugar
½ cup	orange juice
2 tbsp.	cornstarch
1 tsp.	vanilla extract
¼ tsp.	nutmeg
1½ cups	flour
2 tsp.	baking powder
½ tsp.	salt
½ cup	butter *or* margarine, melted
½ cup	milk
1	egg

■ Drain fruit reserving 1½ cups syrup (if necessary, add water to measure 1½ cups).

■ Add ½ cup sugar, orange juice, cornstarch, vanilla and nutmeg. Mix until cornstarch is dissolved.

■ Place fruit in a 13 x 9-inch baking dish. Pour syrup mixture over fruit. Sift together flour, remaining sugar, baking powder and salt.

■ Combine butter, milk and egg; stir in dry ingredients. Spoon batter over fruit.

■ Bake at 400°F, 25 to 30 minutes or until golden brown.

■ Serve warm with ice cream, if desired.

8 servings

Chocolate Pear Tart

1 cup	chocolate cookie crumbs
½ cup	chopped toasted almonds
¼ cup	sugar
⅓ cup	butter *or* margarine, melted
1 pkg.	(6 oz.) semi-sweet chocolate chips
1 tsp.	instant coffee crystals
1 can	(15¼ oz.) DEL MONTE® Bartlett Pear Halves, undrained
1 tsp.	unflavored gelatin
1 cup	whipping cream, whipped to stiff peaks

■ Preheat oven to 350°F. In medium bowl, combine cookie crumbs, almonds and sugar. Stir in butter. Pat into bottom and 1 inch up sides of 9-inch removable-bottom tart pan or pie pan. Bake 8 minutes; cool.

■ In food processor or blender, combine chocolate and coffee; process until fine.

■ Drain pears, reserving ½ cup syrup in small saucepan. Cover and refrigerate pears. Sprinkle gelatin over reserved syrup. Let stand 5 minutes. Bring to boil. Add syrup mixture to chocolate in food processor; process until chocolate melts. Scrape chocolate into medium bowl; fold in whipped cream.

■ Spoon filling into crust. Chill at least 4 hours or until set.

■ Just before serving, carefully cut each pear half lengthwise into ¼-inch thick slices, starting ½ inch from point of pear, leaving pointed end intact. Arrange pears over tart, fanning pears. Garnish with additional cookie crumbs and chopped almonds, if desired.

8 to 10 servings

TIP:

To toast almonds, spread almonds in shallow baking pan. Bake at 350°F, stirring occasionally until crisp and golden brown, about 10 to 15 minutes. For easier cutting, chop almonds while still warm.

Golden Pineapple Carrot Cake

1¾ cups	sugar
1 cup	oil
3	eggs, beaten
1 tsp.	vanilla extract
1 can	(20 oz.) DEL MONTE® Crushed Pineapple, drained
2 cups	grated carrots
2½ cups	flour
1½ tsp.	baking soda
2 tsp.	cinnamon
½ tsp.	nutmeg
½ tsp.	salt
½ cup	chopped pecans

■ Beat together sugar, oil, eggs and vanilla. Mix in pineapple and carrots. Add flour, baking soda, cinnamon, nutmeg and salt; mix well. Stir in nuts. Pour into greased and floured 13 x 9-inch baking dish.

■ Bake at 350°F, 35 to 40 minutes or until tests done; cool. Frost with Cream Cheese Frosting (see recipe below).

12 servings

HELPFUL HINTS:
• *Reserve pineapple juice for other recipe uses.*
• *Recipe may be easily doubled. Bake in two 13 x 9-inch baking dishes. It may be necessary to increase baking time.*

Cream Cheese Frosting

1 pkg.	(8 oz.) cream cheese, softened
¼ cup	butter, softened
2 cups	powdered sugar
1 tsp.	vanilla extract

■ Beat together cream cheese and butter until smooth. Add powdered sugar and vanilla; beat until smooth.

*A*pricot Almond Gelato

2 cups	whipping cream
1 cup	sugar
1 can	(15¼ oz.) DEL MONTE® Apricot Halves, drained
½ cup	lemon juice
¼ cup	apricot brandy
3 tbsp.	chopped almonds, toasted
1 tsp.	vanilla extract
¼ tsp.	almond extract

■ Combine cream and sugar; stir until sugar dissolves.

■ Place fruit in blender container or food processor. Cover and blend until smooth. Add with remaining ingredients to cream mixture; mix until well blended.

■ Pour into freezer-proof container. Cover and freeze overnight.

6 to 8 servings

*S*imply Sorbet

2 cans	(15 oz. *each*) DEL MONTE Fruits in Heavy Syrup
	Flavorings (see variations)

■ About 24 hours ahead, place unopened cans of fruit in freezer.

■ Remove cans from freezer; submerge in hot water about 1 minute. Pour any thawed syrup into full-size food processor bowl (not recommended for mini-processors or blenders). Remove fruit from cans; cut each into eighths.

■ Place frozen fruit chunks into food processor; add flavoring(s). Process until smooth, scraping blade as needed. Serve immediately or spoon into freezer container and store in freezer until ready to use.

7 servings (about ½ cup each)

Variations:

Follow directions above using DEL MONTE Peaches in Heavy Syrup and 1 teaspoon vanilla extract for Peach Sorbet. Use DEL MONTE Pineapple in Heavy Syrup, ⅓ cup well-chilled coconut milk, and, if desired 1 tbsp. rum or rum extract for Piña Colada Sorbet.

Apricot Almond Gelato (left), Easy Peach Sorbet

Easy Peach Sorbet

1 can	(15 oz.) DEL MONTE® Lite Sliced Yellow Cling Peaches
¼ cup	peach schnapps
⅛ tsp.	almond extract

■ Combine undrained peaches with peach schnapps and almond extract in food processor or blender container.

■ Cover and blend until smooth. Pour into freezer-proof container. Freeze until firm, 8 to 10 hours or overnight.

■ Remove from freezer to soften slightly, about 20 to 30 minutes before serving. Scoop to serve.

Makes approximately 1 pint (4 servings)

HELPFUL HINT:
If using a sorbet or ice cream maker, combine ingredients as directed above and process according to manufacturer's instructions.

INDEX

INDEX

INDEX